December 15, 1993

John C. Fitch
Henry Ford Health System
600 Fisher Building
Detroit, MI 48202

Dear John:

If your desk is anything like mine, it already contains more memoranda, letters,
reports, periodicals and books than you can ever expect to read. So why am I sending
you one more? Because every once in a while a piece is written that can positively
impact your workplace. Soar With the Eagles is just that insightful and that powerful
a book. Written by my friend, Chuck Lauer, who is the publisher of Modern
Healthcare, the book contains valuable insights into not only business in general but
specifically into your business and mine, healthcare.

I have shared this book with my management team and they encouraged me to share it
with you. I am convinced that if you will find five minutes to start this book you will
make time to finish it.

At MMBC we look forward to soaring the skies with our healthcare partners.

Best Wishes,

SOAR
WITH THE
EAGLES

By Charles S. Lauer
Publisher, *Modern Healthcare*

CCI BOOKS
A division of Coffey Communications, Inc.
Walla Walla, Washington

Copyright © 1991 by Charles S. Lauer
Printed in the United States of America
All Rights Reserved

May not be reproduced in whole or in part, by any
means, without permission of the publisher.

Library of Congress Catalog Card No. 91-73259

ISBN 0-8163-1061-0

Dedication

To my wife Maggie,
my daughter Kathy,
and my son Randy
—my inspiration and my loves

And to my beloved stepmother,
Dorothy Darché,
who taught me the affection, love,
and gentleness that have served me
so well in all aspects of my life

Acknowledgements

To Gertrude Crain, Keith Crain, and Rance Crain

One of the greatest breaks I have ever had in my life was working for the Crain family, whose support has enabled me to write this book.

I am also deeply indebted to my editor, Barbara Herrera of Coffey Communications, Inc., without whose help, advice, and counsel, my manuscript for this book would never have seen the light of day. She has been my closest adviser in this project.

Contents

SECTION I: MEETING PROFESSIONAL AND EXECUTIVE CHALLENGES

SECTION II: MEETING CHALLENGES IN PEOPLE RELATIONSHIPS

SECTION III: MEETING PERSONAL CHALLENGES

SECTION IV: MEETING MARKETING CHALLENGES

SECTION V: MEETING HEALTHCARE CHALLENGES

From the publisher . . .

Like chickens or turkeys that spend their days scratching the ground in search of anything that looks remotely nourishing, some people pass through life, eyes focused downward, seemingly willing to settle for bits and scraps of happiness and success.

Above them soar the eagles, mounting ever higher on the columns of air that rise from the earth.

In this powerful new book, the publisher of *Modern Healthcare* magazine challenges every reader to declare war on mediocrity—to reject second best, whether in work, relationships, or life itself. Charles S. Lauer believes that success and excellence are within the reach of anyone. He is convinced that not one of us needs be limited in life to scratching with the chickens and turkeys—that the birthright of all of us is instead to soar with the eagles.

Bookstore shelves groan these days under the weight of "success"-oriented books, many of which are well worth reading. But many focus heavily on the "theory" of success—on the "philosophy" of excellence.

In *SOAR WITH THE EAGLES*, you'll find very little theory and philosophy. This is a nuts-and-bolts, practical, rubber-meets-the-road kind of book. Chuck Lauer speaks to you in these pages as if you were sitting across the desk from him. He shares real-life stories and personal convictions, and tells what works and what doesn't in achieving personal and professional success.

Because much of this book first appeared in the popular "Publisher's Letter" column in *Modern Healthcare* magazine, what the author has to say here proceeds quite naturally from his perspective as a leader in the healthcare industry.

But whether your own background as a reader is in healthcare or in another of life's varied pursuits, you will undoubtedly be impressed with the common sense and dis-tilled practical wisdom evident in these pages.

Each chapter in this book is brief—usually no more than two pages in length. And each focuses on a single issue or aspect of the main section heading. Reading these pages, therefore, will not require a tedious effort, but should prove rather to be a satisfying pleasure.

It is our wish that each of you reading this book will truly be motivated to achieve, to succeed, to excel, to do your personal best—to spread your wings and *SOAR WITH THE EAGLES!*

About
Charles S. Lauer . . .

From his position as publisher of *Modern Healthcare* and corporate vice president of Crain Communications in Chicago, Charles S. Lauer has become one of the most respected and sought-after speakers in American business.

His commitments to excellence and client/customer service are the steely threads that link his work as public speaker and as magazine publisher. For *Modern Healthcare*, those commitments have resulted in rebirth. Its experience is one of the great success stories in trade publishing.

The only weekly healthcare business news magazine, *Modern Healthcare* is respected for its bottom-line emphasis, national coverage of management innovations and trends, and tight, readable style.

Its rebirth is credited to Chuck Lauer.

In 1976, Crain Communications purchased *Modern Healthcare* from McGraw-Hill and brought in Lauer to turn it around.

Although the magazine lacked a strong financial base and editorial direction, Lauer gradually helped it to gain both, as well as the trust and respect of the healthcare community—senior executives, legislators, consultants, consumers of healthcare services, manufacturers, and others.

As a result, *Modern Healthcare* is now the premier business news publication for the industry. It is supported by a team of world-class reporters in cities such as Chicago, Dallas, Los Angeles, Washington, and New York. It attracts an expanding circulation of more than 80,000 readers.

Lauer's zeal for clear, focused, and personal communication with readers carries into the relationship he develops with audiences during his speaking engagements. Within a single year, he delivers more than seventy-five speeches and talks to leaders in hospitals and healthcare systems, consultants, vendors, and students.

He addresses the emerging developments in healthcare in terms of their impact on people: business executives, the elderly, women, and families. His gospel of service, quality, cooperation, and listening to customers and colleagues conveys a powerful message.

Chuck Lauer's commitment to journalistic excellence and client/customer service goes back more than thirty years. After military service during the Korean War and graduate work at Northwestern University's Medill School of Journalism, Lauer began his career as a merchandising representative for *Life* during that magazine's heyday. There he developed the belief in customer-focused sales, reader-focused writing, and people-focused speaking which colors all that he addresses today.

At the American Medical Association, he served as general sales manager for the association's fifteen publications, as well as the AMA's director of communications. In addition, he understands the perspective and interests of healthcare consumers from his years as executive vice president of Family Media—publisher of *Family Health* and *1001 Decorating Ideas*. He also held the position of national advertising sales director for Petersen Publishing Company—publisher of *Hot Rod*, *Motor Trend*, *Teen*, and a host of other special-interest consumer publications.

Whether Lauer is chatting with a group of graduate students, participating in a retreat for trustees, or delivering a keynote address to an audience of hundreds of healthcare leaders, he has the unique ability to inform, entertain, and inspire—an ability very much in evidence in the pages just ahead.

Meeting Professional and Executive Challenges

Leaders don't force people to follow—they invite them on a journey.

1

Seize the moment

G ood timing is something that few people understand. Some people have it instinctively, while others work hard and long to earn it. But once you've experienced "the magic of the moment," you begin to realize how critical timing is to personal and business success.

Take a look at the truly successful people you know. Whether they're entrepreneurs, athletes, musicians, technicians, or executives, they generally have a good sense of timing.

Take an even closer look at these individuals and you'll notice something else. They have what some people call "a touch of class." Ever wonder why some people can enter a social event or meeting at just the right moment, while others stumble in to the embarrassment and dismay of everyone? And why is it that some people can tell a funny story and have everyone in the room waiting for the punch line, while others lose the audience halfway through the joke?

The answer is in timing. Although most of us like to think of ourselves as good communicators, many of us fail at the task because we lack a sense of timing. In the healthcare business, for example, healthcare executives, vendors, and consultants often wait around for the right moment. Some are literally frozen in their tracks, waiting for colleagues or competitors to make a strategic move. What they usually discover is that there is no right moment. Now—the present—is usually the best time for risk takers to go after new opportunities and capture key chunks of the market.

2

Dreams are the key to success

One of my favorite magazines has always been *Business Marketing*, published by Crain Communications—the company that also publishes *Modern Healthcare*. Every issue is full of marketing, advertising, and sales guidance that will keep any organization on the track of profitability and success.

In the August 1987 issue of *Business Marketing*, advertising entrepreneur Doug Wilhide wrote an article in which he explained why he had opened his own agency. One sentence within the article caught my attention: "Knowledge and experience tell you all the reasons things can't be done."

In the early phases of a new enterprise, it seems as if nothing is impossible. The opportunities seem boundless, and failure is never an option. Then success comes along and seduces and corrupts us.

Isn't it ironic that swashbuckling executives who often achieved the impossible during a company's growth years become cautious, stodgy, and complacent with time?

Wilhide's remedy for business boredom is simple, but makes good sense. "Think like a kid," he says. "Teach some kids in an advertising course (or selling or marketing): You'll be amazed at how they bring you back to first principles and how they rejuvenate your enthusiasm for the profession."

Sometimes we get so caught up in organizational politics, bureaucratic runarounds, and our own success that we lose sight of the mission, vision, and values of our business. Even more important, we lose sight of who we are as people and as professionals. In short, we abandon our dreams and get diverted from the bold path we had carved for our business and personal lives.

In the end, dreams, spirit, and an abiding belief in the impossible are the essence of a successful life.

3

Stay in touch

M any of my generation remain baffled and bewildered by information systems and computers. Even electronic typewriters strike terror into my heart. In the past thirty-five years, I've done most of my writing hunt-and-peck style on a manual typewriter that would probably qualify as an antique.

Technology has produced some incredible results, but it isn't always the answer to our problems. For example, today's telephone systems perform wonderful feats. In some organizations, computers answer the phone when you fail to dial a person's direct line, and some of them even succeed in making you feel guilty for calling.

Many of these telephone systems were sold to companies on the basis of their potential to save time and cut costs. Unfortunately, some of them do just the opposite.

Are these systems really more efficient than the operators who staffed switchboards and handled every type of call with speed, charm, and a sense of humor? You have to wonder.

Outranking automation as a major business faux pas is the reluctance of many executives to answer their own phones. Everyone has meetings to attend and planes to catch, so there are times when answering your own phone is impractical and impossible. But there's no excuse for executives in sales or service operations to have calls screened by secretaries.

Unfortunately, too many executives consider distance and aloofness to be a part of the senior management mystique. The advice is simple: Top-ranking executives should answer their own phones. Although they'll undoubtedly spend some time weeding out counterfeit characters, they'll also have the opportunity to speak to clients, customers, and patients who want to offer feedback or even do more business. Top executives can't be removed from the action or they may find their boards removing them from their jobs.

In the mid-1980s, a young executive named Michael Rindler took over the almost-bankrupt Beloit Hospital in Beloit, Wisconsin. In just a few years, he made that hospital a dynamic and profitable operation.

One of his first steps was to make himself accessible. To that end, he gave newly admitted patients a card with his office and home phone numbers and asked them to call if they were disappointed or dissatisfied with their treatment.

There's one senior executive who's *involved.*

4

Attitude starts at the top

People's attitudes are *so* important. A positive attitude can increase productivity, while a negative attitude has the opposite effect.

What's termed "corporate culture" usually starts with a company's top officer. If he or she is open, innovative, positive, and full of energy and enthusiasm, that's usually reflected in other employees in the organization. But if the top executive is insular, miserly, autocratic, and devoid of humor and enthusiasm, then those same traits and attitudes usually permeate the company. So to really get a fix on the culture of a company, try to meet the top officer.

A classic example of this is seen at Northwest Airlines. Unfortunately, about all you once heard about Northwest was the tale of the three pilots who allegedly had too much to drink before a flight. That incident has masked an even bigger, more interesting story about the turnaround in attitude at Northwest. Let me explain.

Northwest Airlines has new bosses—and what a change in attitude they brought about in less than a year! Union officers, always ready to fight, now praise the company. So do pilots and cabin crews. People who avoided flying on Northwest now try to schedule themselves on the airline whenever possible; I'm one of them.

But until a few weeks ago I wasn't sure of what had happened at Northwest. Then I read a feature story in *USA Today* about the new owners. Here's what I learned. Northwest's chairman is Alfred Checchi, who learned all about catering to customers at the Marriott Corporation, as did a number of the other new owner-partners of the airline. The new president, Frederick Rentschler, learned his customer service lessons as head of the Beatrice Corporation.

Vice Chairman Fred Malek describes the old corporate attitude at Northwest: "It was authoritarian, penalty-oriented: Sneak up and find someone doing something wrong and discipline them."

This is how he describes the new attitude: "We want to sneak up on people and find them doing something right—and let them know about it."

And what about this? Over the next five years, Northwest will spend over $422 million to improve service, doing things like refurbishing older planes, reducing seats in business class, and giving passengers more and better food. This year alone they'll spend about $866,000 to teach managers and supervisors how to motivate employees and build teamwork. And according to a Northwest spokesman, Mr. Checchi "wants improved employee relations, because he knows you'll get improved customer service."

What about productivity? When the Department of Transportation began reporting on-time records of airlines in 1987, Northwest always ranked as one of the worst. But in the first quarter of the year after their change in ownership, they led the six largest airlines and ranked second overall. And 80 percent of their flights landed right on time. That's quite a turnaround, and it all started at the top with new owners dedicated to customer service and high employee morale.

These same principles apply to any business, whether it sells a product or service, because customer service is the key to success in the 1990s. Chairman Checchi has a five-year plan to make Northwest the preferred airline of them all. If what I hear and read and experience on Northwest is any indication, I think he just might reach his goal.

Attitude is everything, and when the top officers display a positive attitude and take steps to implement their ideals throughout the organization, success and profits usually follow. Companies reflect their management.

5

There's a difference between management and leadership

M any employees who work on their own look forward
to the time when they'll be promoted into management. They work hard and take courses to develop
management skills, and because of their energy and drive,
they're often recognized and promoted into higher-level
positions.

All too often, these aggressive superstars fall flat on their
faces as executives. The reasons aren't that difficult to understand. Although they demonstrate loyalty, high energy, and
goal orientation, many high-achieving staff people were never
cut out to be executives.

Why? Because, in many cases, they can manage, but they
can't lead. There's a difference between leadership and management that many healthcare executives choose to ignore.
While a good manager is methodical, organized, and deliberate, a strong leader is bold, aggressive, and oriented toward
change and action.

Unfortunately, too many organizations put managers in
leadership positions and leaders in management positions.
Although both functions are critical to organizational success,
each demands a different set of attitudes and skills.

Good managers get things done. Patient and encouraging,
they nurture and develop the people who report to them.

Thoughtful and discerning, they tend not to make snap judgments. Moreover, they excel at careful planning and strategizing.

Leaders, on the other hand, are oriented toward the external environment and an ever-growing base of customers. Imaginative and visionary, they rarely let protocol and paperwork get in their way.

Organizations need good managers and good leaders, but don't ever fall into the trap of expecting managers to be leaders and leaders to be managers. Occasionally, you may find a person who fits the bill on both dimensions, but more often than not, you'll need to make allowances for individual differences and help people find an appropriate niche.

6

Delegate, but stay involved

As an organization becomes more successful, the senior executive grows more isolated from the daily business routine.

Although growth demands that senior management delegate line responsibilities, there's a price to be paid for following traditional principles of sound management. When members of the senior management team knock on the executive's door, it's usually to discuss a crisis, problem, or potential pitfall. The result is that the senior executive hears bad news and doom-and-gloom predictions, but little about organizational heroes or victories on the battlefield of business.

Where's the message for healthcare executives? Do everything you can to celebrate your organization's small but unique triumphs. Stay in touch with your organization's personality and character. And make it a habit to travel to the front lines and meet regularly with the troops.

It's no secret: The pace of change within the healthcare industry—as well as within most other industries and businesses—becomes more frantic with every passing year. Only by staying in touch with your people can you keep your finger on the pulse of your organization and your business.

7

Count to ten before you react

One of the great maladies of corporate America is the tendency to fabricate a crisis. Consider this scenario . . . the sales manager of the Haskins Furniture Corporation rushes into the president's office with these words: "The senior VP's secretary at Memorial Hospital just called to say that our toughest competitor, Neal Bonds, is visiting the hospital's purchasing director right now. You know how Bonds operates. He'll give away the farm and undercut the deal we just made with Memorial. I think you should call the purchasing director right now and cut 20 percent off the prices we just quoted him. That way, we'll be sure to keep his business."

And what happens? The president follows the advice of the sales manager and does just that. But then the purchasing director calls: "Funny that you called me right now, because I just threw one of your competitors out of my office. He quoted me a price that was so low that I started to wonder about the quality of his products. But it seems I was wrong, and maybe I should review this whole deal."

Of course, this is a simplistic example, but it's something that happens every day in my business—and perhaps yours too. The sales manager's reaction to a routine piece of desktop gossip was a classic overreaction. And the president's willingness to participate in the panic only escalated the situation.

All of this mania could have been avoided. The sales manager's paranoia had turned a simple phone call into a manufactured crisis. Anxiety and the absence of an overall philosophy to guide decision making can create an environment where crisis and panic are the norm. Employees who are agitated and on edge may produce results in the short term, but they tend to lose business over the long haul.

So the next time someone rushes into your office with a fabricated crisis, try counting to ten, or even twenty, before you act or overreact. You'll probably hold on to your customer's or supplier's business and to your own sanity and self-esteem as well.

8

There are more important things than being well-liked

The president of a prominent healthcare manufacturing firm sadly reported that he had terminated three of his top sales executives. "We've been working with these individuals for some time now—trying to get them to be more confrontational," he said.

"But they couldn't do it, and their sales people never performed up to the levels we expected. If a sales executive can't confront people and let them know what they're doing wrong, their performance falls off."

This problem isn't confined to the profession of sales. In today's "I just want to be liked and loved" society, the ability to constructively criticize another person has fallen out of fashion, and people have suffered as a result of it. It's too easy to pat someone on the back, ignore negative performance, and naively hope that the situation will blow over. But it rarely does.

As a result, people never receive the coaching they need to improve and perform up to expectations. It's great to be liked and have a loyal following of friends and associates. But the reality is that people who set new standards of performance are often the subject of envy, not admiration.

"Do you want to be liked—or do you want to be respected?" is a question you might want to ask yourself when the going gets tough. The sad truth is that likability and respect don't always come as a package; in gaining one, you sometimes surrender the other.

Achieving results—in education, business, relationships, and families—means having the courage to confront and deliver bad news. That's how people grow and reach a position where they can share their knowledge with others. One of life's most fundamental principles is that people need guidance, direction, and leadership. Direct but kindly confrontation is often the first step toward success.

9

Communicate regularly and sustain accountability

Accountability is a way of life in the business world. The chairman of a corporation must report to the stockholders, and even the president of the United States must report to the American people.

Unfortunately, some people feel constrained by reporting relationships, and they resent being held accountable for their actions. These people are usually whining complainers who don't get much accomplished.

Fortunately, the world is full of another brand of individual. People who are winners—who accept life as it comes—like to be held accountable. They want their performance measured and evaluated, and they make sure that their bosses know what they're doing and where they're headed.

Show me employees who fail to communicate, and I'll show you employees who aren't happy with their work. Satisfied, positive people usually share information and stay in touch with their bosses, their colleagues, their secretaries, and most important, with their customers.

Bosses acknowledge and appreciate employees who are good communicators. Ask executives to name their top employees, and you'll hear the names of people who keep management informed and up to date. Top employees who travel extensively tend to call their offices regularly and let others know their whereabouts—just in case their bosses or customers need to get in touch. If bosses start to suspect that employees aren't letting them in on important details, paranoia and distrust set in. For most employees, that's the beginning of the end.

Here's my advice to managers and people on the way up: Learn to communicate, but make it your mission to turn communication with your boss into a fine art. Do this, and your boss will willingly share secrets on how to communicate with clients, customers, and other important publics.

In today's competitive environment, individuals and organizations that subscribe to the code of communication and accountability will have a leg up on competitors.

10

Be a doer—and surround yourself with doers

Not everyone in this country has the same work ethic, but that's what makes life intriguing. Variety—not only in people, but in organizations and ideologies—is indeed the spice of life.

Success and financial rewards also add spice to life. But they rarely come easily and without effort. If they do, there's usually a heavy price to be paid. Unfortunately, people nurtured on a mass-media diet of instant gratification seem to believe that success is a birthright that has little or no relationship to hard work, dedication, and sacrifice.

Not only do they believe that the world, or government, or society owes them a living; they also tend to look down at people who reach their goals through persistence and hard work.

No matter how high I've climbed within publishing organizations, I've always tried to look at myself as an old-fashioned working stiff. That's probably the reason I still consider it a privilege to have a job, make a contribution, and live in a country where the future seems bright and limitless. It also explains why I have such little patience for people whose only loyalty is to themselves and who chronically complain about their employers.

Fortunately, this nation is full of individuals who rally round the flag and make a difference every working day. They give everything they've got to their jobs, and they go the distance to please their customers. Never ones to slack off or get sidetracked by mistakes, they sacrifice and move full speed ahead to deliver on their promises. It's not surprising that they also tend to be the people who earn promotions, awards, and financial gains.

For many people, work is a hobby, a pastime, or a convenient means to a paycheck. But in the coming decades, organizations won't survive without a heavy investment in old-fashioned doers. Smart executives will offset their weaknesses and magnify their strengths by surrounding themselves with colleagues who have a strong belief in hard work and discipline.

11

Control the rumor mill

Rumors can destroy or call into question any relationship. Yet rumors exist within almost every organization, social group, or family.

In the business world, management tends to blame employees for rumors and often ridicules or punishes the individuals who start them. But management often ignores the fact that rumors arise because senior executives have been less than candid with the work force.

Rumors usually begin because people want a greater sense of control over their lives. They throw out an idea to a friend or associate, knowing that it bears little resemblance to the truth. Why? Because they want to feel important. They want to appear as if they know what's going on.

This type of behavior is typical within large and small organizations. The more an organization is going through the pangs of change and growth, the more rumors run rampant. And if an organization is on the block or about to be acquired, the rumor mill becomes almost deadly.

What's the solution? Management must over-communicate with the work force so people understand what's going on. All too often, management views employees not as respected colleagues, but as adversaries. And all too often, parents view their children not as individuals, but as chattel to be controlled.

Usually this is a sign that management—either in business or in the family—is disoriented, weak, and confused about such fundamental issues as mission, vision, and values.

Study any successful organization, social group, or family, and you usually find a high level of communication. Rumors are kept to a minimum, because people in leadership roles have a commitment to keep everyone informed. They realize that it's natural and normal for others to want to know what's going on. So instead of ridiculing questions, they provide clear and immediate answers. As a result, people feel recognized and valued.

The next time you hear a rumor, take a hard look at yourself and the people around you. To what extent have you contributed to their feeling of confusion and frustration? Remember, they're usually interested in knowing what's going on.

12

Be accessible

T he telephone is one of the most important tools of the publishing trade. It helps us keep in touch with customers, colleagues, creditors, secretaries, and family members.

I've probably spent as much time on the telephone as on airplanes—and I travel a couple hundred thousand miles a year. As a self-styled telephone expert, here's my advice for making it work for your organization:

✦ Answer your own phone. Consultants tell us that executives who answer their own phones are wasting time that should be invested in holding meetings or writing memos. But maybe the reason that so many executives are out of touch with the market is that they've avoided talking to clients, colleagues, and customers.

✦ View telephone conversation as a learning experience. Usually when someone wants to talk to me, it's because they're interested in my business and my publication— and, after all, that's what I'm being paid to talk about. But even more important, I've discovered that I almost always learn something from a telephone conversation—or at least I retrieve a new contact or sales lead.

✦ Keep in mind that when you answer the telephone, you project an instant image of your organization to the other party. I wonder how some of us would react if we could hear ourselves at the other end of the line? For starters, try taping some of your telephone conversations and playing them back. You'll be amazed at the results. All too often, receptionists, secretaries, administrative assistants, and even managers have little or no training in telephone courtesy. Just remember that neglecting or minimizing this vital skill can create long-term problems for your organization.

+ Pick up the telephone for your colleagues and associates. People who refuse to extend this courtesy aren't just exhibiting arrogance and bad manners; they're undermining your business.

+ Invest in telephone training. If people receive the proper training, they perform according to expectations. But all too often, management looks at telephone training in the same way they look at business manners and etiquette. They assume that everyone knows how to behave from experience and training in the home. Of course, we all know that isn't the case. Sales have been won and lost on the basis of how a telephone is answered.

13

Actions speak louder than words

More people are talking about such concepts as honor, integrity, and taking full responsibility for one's actions. Unfortunately, in all too many cases, that's all it is—a lot of talk.

Although people eagerly accept responsibility during the good times, they're less than enthusiastic about assuming blame when things go south. Executives who failed to achieve company goals bail out with "golden parachutes" and pursue comfortable lifestyles. Ask many of these executives about their resignations, and they're quick to put the blame on everyone but themselves.

But this wasn't the approach taken by Reverend Colin Buchanan, formerly the Bishop of Aston in Birmingham, England. In an attempt to stage a series of events honoring Archbishop Desmond Tutu of South Africa, the reverend persuaded church elders to advance money for promotion and hall and equipment rentals. He expected 90,000 people to buy tickets, but when only 13,000 showed up, the church lost more than $300,000.

Although people initially poked fun at the reverend's naivete, they changed their attitude when he accepted full responsibility for what had happened and then resigned as Bishop of Aston. A columnist for *The Times of London* echoed the feelings of many people when he wrote that Bishop Buchanan "has put back squarely before us the concept of responsibility and done so in the most striking manner possible—that is, by accepting responsibility openly and without qualification."

In reflecting on his decision, Reverend Buchanan said, "I didn't spend my time saying, 'What have other people got away with?' All I know is that this was the decision I had to make at that particular moment. Really, it's just like a child owning up to something in school."

Think of the hearts that have been broken, the careers destroyed, the lives disrupted, and the billions of dollars lost because people refuse to accept responsibility. Executives of Exxon seemed to blame everyone but themselves for the massive oil spill off the coast of Alaska. Instead of relying on such traditional virtues as candor, directness, and common sense, these executives seemed to have all their moves orchestrated by a bevy of lawyers.

But there is an alternative—even on the corporate level. When cyanide poisoning killed seven people in 1982, Johnson & Johnson Chairman James Burke immediately pulled Tylenol off the shelves. There was no second-guessing or side-stepping of responsibility. Johnson & Johnson simply took action. The incident is now a textbook example of how one corporation called on its most basic values and produced a positive response from both consumers and the media.

Personal honor, integrity, and honesty are characteristics that we admire in leaders and in organizations that we choose to patronize. But all too often, people who make impassioned public pleas for our respect and trust fail to back up their words with actions. Behaving honorably is just one more way of treating people right.

14

Take your time deciding about people

When I first started selling advertising, my colleagues told me that the advertising manager of a Fortune 500 corporation was a terror who continually refused to see anyone from our sales force.

The story was that my company had fired someone whom the advertising manager admired and that since that time he had held a grudge against us. Even back then, I was a stubborn sort who enjoyed making up my own mind about people.

So one day, I called the advertising manager and tried to sell him a special position in the magazine. To my surprise, he was gracious and charming. He told me he appreciated my call and the invitation to buy a special position. After several days, he called me back with a large contract.

How many times have you heard that the guy two floors down is a jerk—or that the woman who lives two blocks away can't get along with anyone? But what happens when you meet the person? Usually, you discover that your assessment of the person is in total contrast with what you've heard. And more often than not, you end up liking the person about whom you heard so many contemptible things.

The point of this is simple: Don't let people's opinions of others sway you until you've had an opportunity to judge for yourself. Customers, clients, colleagues, acquaintances, and strangers on the street are people—the same as you and me. Some are easier to get along with than others, but if you're willing to spend the time and energy, everyone can be known and understood. Someone who's earned a reputation for being "tough" and "difficult" usually wants to do an extraordinarily good job and therefore has set high personal standards for performance. People who want to sustain a relationship over the long haul understand this and press on.

If you're like me, you'll probably discover that the people who initially give you the most trouble are also the ones you end up admiring.

15

Brevity is a part of good manners

Brevity, in my opinion, is critically important in relationships with other people, and any executive or salesperson who doesn't understand this concept won't be very successful. That means brevity in written as well as verbal communication, but some people seem oblivious to time when dealing with other people.

Some individuals are so caught up in what they want to say that they don't appreciate the time it takes others to read a memo or listen to a rambling monologue. Sometimes we call them bores, and other times they're branded as stupid. Either way, it's sad.

Learning how to say and write things succinctly is critical to success, but too many people just haven't been properly trained. Let's start with memos. Most memos I get take about three or four paragraphs to say something that should only take about two sentences.

The problem is that some people seem to believe that the more they put into a memo, the more impressive it is. But that's not the purpose of a memo. Memos are meant to inform and get people to take action.

The same goes for sales letters. Make them short and to the point, and be considerate of other people's time. Good sales letters are not exercises in English composition. Try to write as you speak. Trying to sound like an English professor makes your letters awkward and stilted. And anyway, most English professors aren't particularly good at sales.

And then there's verbal communication. Again, get to the point. I tell all my salespeople that they should be able to tell our sales story in five minutes. Now, that isn't easy, and it takes practice. But it pays off.

Clients and prospects have the same time constraints you have. They have plenty of pressures on them, and the last thing they need is some windbag wasting their time. But a lot of salespeople and others have never gotten the message, and thus they can't understand why it's so difficult for them to get appointments.

It all boils down to this: Learn how to say what you have to say without a lot of excess verbiage. Be sensitive to other people's time to a fault. If someone wants to engage you in a more lengthy discussion, let them invite you to do so. And, as a matter of fact, if what you have to say at the beginning of a dialogue is concise and engaging, the other person will probably want you to stay longer. But that doesn't mean you've got all the time in the world.

Always assume the other person has only one or two minutes to hear your pitch. Practice saying what's essential in a few words. It's great discipline, and believe me, as you learn how to do this, you will be encouraged by the response you get from people. In many cases they will actually seek you out, because they know you won't waste their time.

Finally, think of the concept of brevity with people as a part of good manners. When you don't impose on other people's time, you are showing respect and good manners. Most of the time it also shows that you know what you're talking about.

Was I brief enough?

16

Learn to adjust to the competition

Competition can bring out the best in people—or their worst. Despite its liabilities, competition is vital. Without it, people would grow lazy and complacent. No one would be motivated to strive for growth and excellence.

Successful people thrive on competition and look forward to their next competitive bout. Others tend to panic—usually because they haven't taken the time to look ahead, anticipate future market forces, and develop a game plan, including the arrival of new competitors.

The best and strongest defense against competition is staying in touch with clients and customers. If a competitor comes on the scene, you're more likely to learn about it if you're in contact with the people you serve. In most cases, telephone calls are rarely adequate to wage war on the competition. In the end, there's no substitute for eyeball-to-eyeball interaction and a healthy exchange of ideas.

And what if you find yourself being criticized by competitors? Consider it a compliment, give thanks, and keep your mouth shut. Most top-performing executives and organizations don't waste any time knocking their competitors. In fact, people tend to get turned off if you look like you have nothing better to do than slam other people and organizations.

But learning to thrive on competition in a competitive world is no easy task. Healthcare executives who have increased their market share did so with solid market research and planning. Their less-successful colleagues elected to blame everything and everybody—from Medicare reimbursement and physicians, to fussier patients and technology—for their problems. In many cases, blaming and passing the buck is a convenient cover for poor planning, management, and evaluation.

17

Make integrity
a way of life

Y ou've heard people say it: "I like doing business with that company, because it gives you a square deal." "I like dealing with her, because she has a way of treating people right." "He's the kind of guy you can trust."

Think of the people and organizations you enjoy doing business with and ask yourself why. Usually it's because of their honesty and integrity. Numerous studies suggest that people will pay more for a product if they trust the company to provide excellent service and follow-up.

More than any other characteristic, integrity is the barometer for success in corporate America. Without integrity, few executives last very long. Neither their employees nor their clients and customers will trust them. It's easy to compromise your principles, but usually there's a price to be paid. And more often than not, that price is disgrace, business failure, and public humiliation.

Integrity is equally evident in the way people and organizations treat competitors or personal rivals. Many organizations train sales and marketing executives to put down competitors. But you have to wonder about people who invest more time in dishing out verbal right hooks than promoting products, services, and achievements.

If you call attention to competitors or rivals, you give them visibility and free promotion. And keep in mind that most Americans have soft spots in their hearts for underdogs. If they hear you denigrate another person or organization, they just might spring to their defense.

One thing is sure: People and organizations that earn the respect of others exude integrity. They're so involved in living and in enjoying other people that they don't have time for petty scraps and character assassination. Integrity is as much a part of their personal lives as their professional lives. No matter where they are or who they're with, they keep their word, come to the aid of others, and play life straight.

Integrity is basic to personal and professional success. It demands a commitment not just to talking about honesty and integrity but to living these values every day of the year.

18

Take time from your busy schedule to read

Many of us who work for a living are on the fast track. Time flies, and before we know it, we have none left. Between handling crises, rushing to meetings, and checking our mail, we get so caught up in our daily routine that we lose perspective on our industry and on the world around us.

The solution isn't in catching up with a half hour of television news, which typically excludes too much and explains too little. Neither can we go back to the days when we were able to spend two hours poring over the morning newspaper.

But two ingredients are indispensable to personal and business success: solitude, and the self-discipline to stay informed and up to date.

We need to set aside specific times of the day when we can invest time in contemplation and study. Professional and personal decisions made without careful thought and examination of available options are usually negative decisions, with disastrous results.

Several decades ago, when I began my career in publishing, I quickly learned that top performers had two distinct reading habits: They read everything they could about their industries, and they read everything—from brochures and newsletters to annual reports and memos—about their clients and customers. When they called on clients and customers, the benefits were obvious: These representatives understood their products and how these products could serve clients' needs.

Successful people take time away from their busy schedules to think, prioritize, and bring themselves up to date on what's happening in the world. If you let yourself get out of touch with the people in your life—whether they're customers, friends, or family members—you're going to lose out.

19

Approach life and work with a spirit of adventure

The things that James Ryder has done in his fifty-six years in the business world would fill volumes. In 1933, Ryder was a Miami construction worker who put down thirty-five dollars on a Ford Model A truck and started hauling debris for local construction crews.

Over the next forty-five years, he built Ryder Systems, Inc. into a half-billion-dollar company that was the nation's leader in truck leasing.

But things took a turn for the worse in the mid-seventies. After some questionable diversification moves and a $20 million dollar loss in the 1974 recession, the company asked James Ryder to retire.

Upon retirement, he had $10 million in stock, a waterfront mansion in Coral Gables, and a 147-foot yacht. In addition, the company offered him a lifetime consulting contract at $100,000 per year if he agreed not to start a competing business.

Instead, James Ryder took $12 million of his total net worth of $15 million, borrowed $260 million from truck manufacturers like Ford and Chrysler, and started a company called Jartran, which competed head-on with Ryder and U-Haul. In two years, he put 30,000 trucks on the road and was the third-largest truck leasing company in the country.

But in 1984, things once again took a turn for the worse. U-Haul slashed its prices and won a $40 million judgment against Jartran. Ryder sold his company for $200,000, and in 1986, Jartran permanently closed its doors.

Since the early 1980s, Ryder has entered the motorboat rental business, a phone-in classified advertising service, a freight brokerage, and mobile-home park development. But all of these businesses failed, and soon James Ryder was down to his last $250,000. He had already sold his yacht and was unable to pay the upkeep on his palatial home. In a goodwill gesture, Ryder Systems, Inc. bought the mansion and allowed Ryder to live in it rent free.

But James Ryder didn't stop there. He invested $240,000 in an international automobile sales and service network. Asked why he didn't give up a long time ago, he replied, "What would I have accomplished that way? Granted, I haven't enjoyed my reverses, but I sure don't want them to make me too conservative."

Ryder is the kind of person who keeps this nation's economy prospering and growing. He's his own man, and he typifies the rough-and-tumble spirit that has made this nation a leader in business and entrepreneurship. James Ryder took his chances and accepted his losses. And never did he come to the federal government in search of a bailout.

20

Hard work improves your odds

This country is filled with people who take on incredible odds, persevere, and win. Triumph over adversity is a persistent theme in American culture that hearkens back to the days of the pilgrims.

Desperate, and driven from their own country, these seventeenth-century freedom fighters clung to their dreams and succeeded in establishing a new life and a new world.

Juanita Crabb is a case study in American courage. Elected as mayor of Binghamton, New York, at the age of 31, she inherited a city that was almost bankrupt and headed for disaster. A born-and-bred Binghamtonian who's also the mother of two teenagers, she spent more than ten years and three terms of office putting the city on a sound financial footing. Her efforts paid off.

In January 1988, the city received runner-up honors in a financial leadership competition co-sponsored by the U.S. Conference of Mayors. And now, instead of leaving Binghamton for Boston, New York, or Chicago, young people have decided to give it another chance.

Giving people a chance is what Juanita Crabb and the Binghamton miracle are all about. Several years ago, Ms. Crabb invited the head of a popular chain of stores called Boscov's to open a store in Binghamton. The initial answer was no, but Ms. Crabb persisted. She sent gifts to Boscov's corporate headquarters in Reading, Pennsylvania.

First it was a dozen roses and then a mug with the inscription, "Long distance relationships are hard." Then, for several weeks, Ms. Crabb sent Boscov's a piece of a jigsaw puzzle which, when completed, formed the outline of a downtown Binghamton department store. The last piece of the puzzle was a sign for the roof, which read "Boscov's."

Her persistence paid off. "She really romanced the company," said a Boscov spokesman. "She's creative and has a lot of imagination, but basically she's a competent administrator."

Despite impossible odds, Mayor Crabb persevered. She never abandoned her dreams, and now she has the pleasure of watching them unfold before her eyes.

21

Never take anything for granted

Never assume anything—from taking care of details and keeping customers, to maintaining a strong relationship with your spouse and family members.

What's my advice? Make sure that what was supposed to happen actually happens. Check to see if your clients or customers still favor your organization and intend to act on their commitment.

Forget the assumption that love is invincible. Instead, communicate your love each day through your words and actions.

Reflect on your own mortality and the fragility of good health. Do whatever you can to keep your body in top form.

In business, taking things for granted is the kiss of death. Too many people make appointments and then forget to confirm the day before. They forget the realities of life—that unexpected emergencies, phone calls, illness, or hastily called meetings can throw anyone's schedule off.

Similar problems occur when we assume that customers will purchase our products and service, patronize our organization, or attend special events. Often we discover that promises made thirty to sixty days ago turn into vague memories.

That's why it doesn't hurt to follow this advice: When someone promises to purchase your products and services or to follow up on a commitment, practice a little healthy paranoia, and assume the worst. Assume that the competition is waiting in the wings—ready to make your client or customer a better offer.

The same lesson applies to personal relationships. Just think how many marriages have shattered and how many children have lost their way because men and women took each other for granted. People become so preoccupied with their careers and social calendars that they forget the transforming power of simple words and phrases such as "Thank you for helping me," "I want you to know how much that means to me," and, of course, "I love you."

And then there's the phenomenon of taking your career and position for granted. Terminated executives spend months—even years—trying to overcome the trauma of being let go after years of dedicated service. In many cases, these executives had stopped innovating and developing themselves and their people years ago. But they still expected their organizations to provide them with a paycheck—just for showing up each day.

We need to spend more time reflecting on the privileges in our life—the privilege of employment, the privilege of having a fulfilling family or personal life, the privilege of freedom and good health, and the privilege and joy of just being alive.

22

Turn a deaf ear to the siren call of mediocrity

Television sports announcers have been known to say, "This game is only a matter of inches." The game of life isn't much different, although many people fail to see it that way.

These are the people you're likely to hear asking: "What difference does it make if I cheat on my expense account?" "What difference does it make if I don't make that call?" "What difference does it make if I call in sick?" "What difference does it make if I don't go back to the office?"

This "so what" school of thinking is the siren call of mediocrity and usually separates the winners from the losers. But who's to blame for these detached, uncaring attitudes?

Usually, management bears at least some of the responsibility. Business is full of executives who love to write memos and reports, schedule and attend meetings, and keep piles of papers in neat stacks. They also tend to be preoccupied with the size and position of their offices and the number of people who report to them. These executives usually care more about feeding their egos and moving their careers along than sound management.

Employees rarely need more than a few weeks to figure out their boss's mode of operation before disillusionment and the "so what" attitude start to set in. Whether they're leading a troop of Girl Scouts or a multimillion-dollar corporation, quality leaders care more about their people than they do about themselves. But in many companies leadership is left to chance. Some executives insist that leadership skills are unteachable, even though organizations such as the U.S. Marine Corps have trained officers to worry about their people first.

The payoff is significant: The esprit de corps in the U.S. Marine Corps is legendary throughout the world. Winning in business and in life demands people who care about what they do. To that end, make sure that the important people in your life understand the myriad ways they can make a difference. Care for others, and you'll be a winner—not by inches, but by miles.

23

Fall in love with your work

Imagine San Francisco quarterback Joe Montana walking off the field in the middle of the Superbowl. Even if he's doing it because the coach—for some good reason unknown to most everyone else—has sent in a new quarterback, most of the fans wouldn't understand.

Whether their game is football or business, good competitors live for the heat and joy of going head-to-head with their compatriots. Unfortunately, a growing number of people feel they were put on this earth to plan for retirement and next winter's vacation.

This is an attitude I've never been able to understand. I've always found it difficult to walk away from my work or my customers for extended periods of time without feeling concerned and even a little guilty. It may be a curse that smacks of being a workaholic, but it also emanates from a sincere love of my work.

Vacations are necessary to replenish the soul and to reestablish your sense of perspective. But I've always viewed them, not as a utopian experience, but as a short-term respite from something I truly enjoy.

Many of the people I know and admire feel much as I do. They're solid performers who make things happen. Their jobs have a high priority in their lives, because they feel privileged and blessed to have a profession and a well-paying position. They've invested hours counseling friends and colleagues who were terminated because of office politics or corporate takeovers, so they understand how much employment contributes to a sense of well-being and self-esteem.

Retirement has never been something that I've looked forward to with zest and enthusiasm. After all, if you truly love your work, why look forward to not doing it? Many people are amazed to discover that life on the tennis court or golf course is not what they had anticipated. Unfortunately, too many business people are sentenced to an unwanted life of leisure by antiquated human resources policies or by corporate mergers or downsizing.

If you live for vacations and look forward to retirement, even though you've just begun your career, don't apply for positions in healthcare management or in sales and marketing. These aren't just jobs—they're commitments. And they deserve our full attention.

Meeting Challenges in People Relationships

People like to be treated with dignity and respect, and if they are, they'll practically break down the door to do business with you.

"

24

Learn to get along with people

After graduating from college in 1952, I was drafted into the U.S. Army. Because my college didn't have ROTC units, I went in at the low rank of private E-2.

I often look back at the two following years as one of the greatest adventures of my life. Why? Because I learned to get along with all kinds of men who hadn't had the opportunity to attend fancy private schools or upscale liberal arts colleges. In the process, I developed a greater appreciation of what people are all about.

In those days, every draftee went through sixteen weeks of basic training. My fellow soldiers were from the hills of West Virginia, the farms of Tennessee, and from hard-edged cities such as Boston and New York. Thrown together in a barracks, we had to form into a team overnight.

There were arguments, threats, and brawls as differences in culture, education, and race surfaced. But eventually, we came together as a unit—largely because there was no other choice.

Students who graduate from prep school, college, or business school may never experience the challenge of having to get along with people of different cultures, races, and socioeconomic backgrounds. Instead of learning cooperation and camaraderie, many of these young people learn arrogance, selfishness, and manipulation.

People in this society need to appreciate and value others—

their needs, wants, preferences, and unique perspective on the world. That's why future executives should never be reluctant to meet the service people who make business run and learn the nitty-gritty of delivering products and services.

Perhaps some graduate schools of business or healthcare management should develop specialized curricula in getting along with people and frontline workers. Then, when people entered the business world as managers and executives, they would acknowledge and appreciate the secretaries, mail clerks, receptionists, food handlers, and assembly line workers who make companies prosper.

Two years in the United States Army taught me a lot about human relationships. In many ways, it helped me to become a better salesman, a better publisher, and a better man. The guys in that barracks will never know it, but they changed my attitude toward human relationships forever.

25

Technology, buildings, and furniture are no substitute for people

I n late 1986 and early 1987, General Motors spent $40 billion buying the most advanced robotics and automation equipment. But the results of using these new gadgets have been mixed.

For example, GM was stunned to discover that its Chevrolet Nova plant, run jointly with Toyota in Fremont, California, is one of its most efficient but least automated plants.

Similar lessons have been learned within the healthcare business. In 1987, William Knaus, M.D., of George Washington University Medical Center, released a study of intensive care units at thirteen major hospitals.

After adjusting outcomes to reflect severity of illness, Dr. Knaus discovered at least one hospital where the death rate was 58 percent higher than anticipated. Surprisingly, the higher death rate was not because of poor technology, but because doctors and nurses worked in an "atmosphere of distrust."

In the top-ranked hospital, where results were 59 percent better than anticipated, doctors and nurses worked as members of a team. If problems arose, nurses had the authority to act on their own.

What do the worlds of automobiles and intensive care have in common? The words *trust, dignity, responsibility*, and *team-*

work come to mind. Without them, the finest information and communications system on the planet won't make a difference. If people aren't properly trained, motivated, and supervised, the world's best product line will never fulfill its potential.

The bottom line is that people really do make a difference. Fancy office furniture and automation mean nothing if workers feel ignored or abused. If General Motors executives had studied the work habits of their employees, perhaps their extravagant investment in automation would have been unnecessary. Teamwork may not mean life and death, but it can dictate an organization's success or failure.

26

Remember who and what you're here for

W ith more than 2,000 beds, Baptist Memorial Hospital in Memphis is the world's largest private hositai. In 1987, I attended Baptist Memorial's seventy-fifth anniversary celebration.

More than 500 people—physicians, healthcare executives, nurses, and business leaders—gathered at the famed Peabody Hotel in Memphis, Tennessee, for the evening's festivities. The ballroom fairly bristled with nostalgia and good feelings—especially for such individuals as Pat Groner, president emeritus of Baptist Memorial, and Joe Powell, Baptist's current president.

Later in the evening, a film especially produced for the event documented Baptist Memorial's achievements over the decades. It was a four-star production, but there was one line spoken by the hospital's pastor that touched me deeply.

"Touch a person with love and respect, and there is much less pain," he said.

Later that evening, I learned that the words had first been uttered by a recovered alcoholic who wanted to pay tribute to the caring members of Baptist Memorial's healthcare team.

"Touch a person with love and respect, and there is much less pain."

For healthcare professionals, that sentence really says it all. But how many of us take the time and trouble to show our love and respect to family members, business associates, and customers? It's admittedly difficult, and it takes time and energy, but it's essential for anyone who deals with people and who wants to inspire others to give freely of their own love and respect.

27

Position your organization for success

To quote the title of a popular Tom Peters book, the healthcare industry needs to discover how it can go on "thriving on chaos."

Instead of allowing the market to dictate how the organization is structured, executives must anticipate and capitalize on market opportunities. That means not waiting for things to happen, but making things happen.

Success stories abound in every industry. Some companies are so lean and mean that they generate energy and movement within a market even though that market is technically in a downswing. According to Peters, successful firms of the future will have these characteristics:

✦ Flatter—with no more than five layers of management

✦ Populated by more autonomous units

✦ Oriented toward differentiation

✦ Producing high-value goods and services

✦ Creating niche markets

✦ Quality- and service-conscious

✦ Increasingly responsive

✦ Faster at innovation

✦ Users of flexible, highly trained people to add value

But underlying all of this is an even more fundamental attribute: a focus on people-to-people relationships within and outside the organization. After all, how can employees be motivated to make a positive impression on external parties unless they first feel committed to the organization's success?

What's the bottom line? Peters explains it in this quote: "The customer responsiveness prescriptions add up to a revolution in corporate life—the wholesale external orientation of everyone in the firm, the achievement of extraordinary flexibility in response to what in the past had been called customer whims."

So if you want to maximize your opportunities for success, don't just pay attention to your customers—make them your life's mission.

28

Invest in people

High-achieving business executives often make mistakes and fail, but those who remain on top are unique: No matter how many times they fail, they have an uncommon ability to rebound and come back fighting.

Making mistakes and chalking up defeats is painful for most executives, but few would deny that failure has been one of the great teachers of their business careers. And most would acknowledge that failure is inevitable. Any executive who makes things happen has to make mistakes and experience backslides and downturns. The reality is that the only way you can avoid mistakes and disappointment is to sit back and do nothing.

It's unfortunate that executives are often so overwhelmed with personal and business concerns that they fail to invest time in the work force. In some cases, they go out of their way to make employees feel bad about their performance, and more important, to feel bad about themselves. The result, of course, is diminished productivity, low morale, cynicism, and high rates of turnover.

The problem is especially acute in large corporations where the competition for promotions is so stiff that executives invest more time in political dogfights than in listening to people's needs.

Why can't business executives remember that people are the most important ingredient and the greatest asset within any organization? Equipment and furniture can be easily refurbished or replaced, but the people who make a business work are precious and unique assets. Taking care of people—whether they happen to be your employees or your customers—is simply good business.

When all is said and done, successful providers, vendors, and consultants share two things in common: high staff morale and an open, caring attitude by senior management.

29

Recognize and appreciate people while they're still around

In the late 1970s, Vi Albrecht's husband, Ralph, died at the age of 78. You could often spot him puttering around and doing repairs—all to make sure that their home and yard stayed in beautiful condition.

Filled with flowers, a rock garden, a weeping willow, and many birds, the back yard was where Vi and Ralph spent some of their happiest moments together. On many spring and summer evenings, you could see them sitting on their screened porch, surrounded by the beauty they had created.

Ralph Albrecht was the kind of man who made you feel richer for having known him. If he knew you were working on a new project around the house, he suddenly appeared to offer support and advice. He was a kind and gentle man, and that's what I told his family at the memorial service that was fittingly held in the garden he had created.

After Ralph died, Vi became a recluse. For the first time in her life, she was alone in the house that she and Ralph had shared for more than fifty years—a house filled with memories of love and joy as well as tears, pain, and disappointment.

She left the house only to get groceries and spent little time in the garden. At night she sat alone in her living room reading or watching television. Her children—who now had children of their own—would occasionally come to the house, and sometimes she would visit them, but never for very long.

The four years following Ralph's death weren't kind to Vi. One night she broke her leg and lay on the floor for almost a full day before someone discovered her. The leg never healed properly, and from that point on, Vi checked in and out of hospitals. Her children tried to convince her to go to a rehabilitation facility, but Vi wanted to stay close to home.

One hot summer day in 1989, one of Vi's neighbors found her in the kitchen, but this time, she was too weak to get up. The neighbor thought Vi had lost her will to live, and she was probably right. One week later, Vi died alone in a hospital room.

Vi won't be coming home anymore, and she'll never know how much I'll miss her. I'll miss waving to her when I pass her living room walking my dog. Although our talks were brief and infrequent, we always waved to each other. I counted on seeing the light in her window at night. She had become an integral part of my life.

Like Vi's other neighbors, I understood her wish to remain at home. For Vi, home was security and memory—a place where she could be surrounded by the things that she and Ralph had accumulated over a lifetime of living together.

Vi won't be coming home anymore, but if you believe in God, you know that Ralph and Vi are together again.

People like Vi can be found all over the country. They confound friends, family members, neighbors, and healthcare experts by insisting on their right to live and die in their own homes. Their decisions may not make economic or medical sense, but then we have to wonder how we would respond when confronted with the same situation.

People like Vi often have little left in their lives but their homes and memories. A smile, wave, or a kind word can go a long way toward making their lives less lonely.

30

Recognize and appreciate people in service jobs

Across our nation, jobs are begging for people to fill them. From counter people at fast-food restaurants and gas station attendants, to janitors and taxicab drivers, these jobs typically involve waiting on people and rendering service.

Unemployment may be serious in some regions of this country, but how many service jobs go unfilled? And how many of the so-called unemployed pursue these jobs?

The life of a service worker is far from glamorous. Many of these jobs are simplistic, dull, and feature starting pay that rarely goes above the minimum wage. Service jobs offer an honest living, but many young people view them with arrogance and disdain. Waiting on people and offering fast, efficient, polite service is somehow perceived as being "beneath" them.

But why? American society has put so much emphasis on glamorous, lucrative executive positions that young people grow up feeling like they'll be branded as failures if they choose to wait on others. Those who chose a service occupation are often robbed of their dignity and sense of professionalism.

In addition, young people have few positive role models for service professions. Stereotypes perpetuated by television and films only accentuate the problem.

Neverthless, we all know of people who wait on tables, pump gas, drive cabs, and care for patients who make their mortgage payments, rear good kids, and generally make a solid contribution to society. In fact, the argument could be made that service professionals make this society work in a way that could never be equaled by high-powered executives in Brooks Brothers suits.

The real tragedy is that young people are alienated by service occupations in the midst of a booming service economy. Where will we find people to perform the jobs critical to making this economy flourish?

Perhaps we need to reexamine our culture's value system and help people understand that you needn't be a jet-setting corporate executive, musician, or million-dollar ball player to be viewed by your peers as a success.

The world is full of service people, and unless we can make them feel good about themselves and the jobs they perform, we may end up with severe and unanticipated personnel shortages.

31

Remember the people you love and care about

F ew things are as important as the family. Giving love, attention, security, and shelter to those we care about is the essence of life.

Some people internalize this message at an early age, while others spend decades caught in selfish games and material pursuits. Some individuals who have never known a family long for its joy and sustenance, while others blithely take family members for granted and ignore their needs.

Late in 1988, I was invited to address the sales force of a company that was in the process of being sold. Instead of facing an audience of despondent, demoralized people, I was greeted by a sea of smiling faces.

The reasons became quickly apparent. The senior executives of this enlightened company had faced up to their responsibilities. Instead of letting their employees flounder, they had invited in numerous external experts to address various aspects of corporate acquisitions.

But the talk was not all business. One of the speakers was a psychologist who specialized in working with companies in the process of acquisition or takeover. Speaking in rich detail about families, he stated that whatever happens to us in the work force also affects our spouses, children, and loved ones. He said that when we go through bad times, the people around us usually feel the same emotions and experience the bad time with us.

"Your family feels everything you do," he told the audience, "but sometimes they're forgotten or left out of the equation." The same principles apply to the world of work. If the leader, senior executive, manager, or supervisor is positive and upbeat about the challenges ahead, most employees will pick up at least some of that zeal and enthusiasm for the task at hand. But if the boss is negative, cynical, or despairing over the future, employees will internalize many of the same attitudes in their work.

Keep in mind that whatever affects you also affects those around you. No matter what the nature of your private pain, remember that the people around you need your love, support, and understanding. Never be afraid to let those who care for you know about your problems and concerns.

Sharing is what love and friendship are all about.

32

Don't judge books
by their dust jackets

Every Saturday morning, I have lunch in a restaurant in
my hometown. The woman who typically waits on me
is about 27 years old—the same age as my daughter. Her
broad smile and bright sense of humor always make me feel
welcome. And she's so clever with words that she usually talks
me into some pie à la mode for dessert.

I eventually learned that she had two children and had been
married to a man who had made her feel bad about herself.
"He was always criticizing me because I hadn't graduated
from high school and didn't have a college degree," she said.

But now things were different. She was married to a man
who gave her the confidence and support she needed to tackle
the rigors of daily life.

Why does this woman offer a lesson to us? Although high
school diplomas and college and graduate degrees have value,
a person with none of these credentials still has worth. When
I was stationed in Korea with the U.S. Army, I learned a
valuable lesson: The men with extensive formal education
weren't always the best soldiers, and many men with four-star
educational credentials had poor attitudes and little common
sense or street smarts.

But all too often we evaluate people on the basis of their
educational credentials—not on who they are and what
they've done with their lives. Many jobs require people who
possess two basic attributes: A desire to work, and a desire to

persevere with a task or assignment. People who have had to struggle through life are often better motivated and better suited to their jobs than others who are more sophisticated or have better educations. Instead of interpreting, analyzing, and evaluating assignments, these graduates of the school of hard knocks go out and do their jobs—and they're thrilled to have been given the opportunity.

Intelligence, warmth, a willingness to give 100 percent, and integrity are what make things happen in business and in life. Many people who are working as secretaries, mail room clerks, or receptionists would welcome the opportunity to grow as people and as professionals. And they would probably dazzle organizations with their contributions.

I speak from personal experience. One of the best sales-people that *Modern Healthcare* ever had was a secretary with a high school diploma. All she needed was training and encouragement to feel good about herself and what she could offer the organization.

Giving people an opportunity to advance and move up and live better, more satisfying lives is what this country is all about. No matter how schooled we become, we can never overlook the gold mine of simple, good-hearted, and talented people who need a break.

33

Care for the caregivers

In many—not all, but many—healthcare organizations, nurses are dissatisfied with their wages, working conditions, opportunities for advancement, and the treatment they receive from physicians and healthcare executives.

The ongoing nursing shortage and problems in retention, productivity, and morale make nursing one of the most critical human resources issues for the 1990s. The problem of nurse recruitment and retention has been growing for decades. Although some healthcare executives successfully ignored the crisis for years, it shows no sign of disappearing or even abating.

Unfortunately, the mass media never explored the plight of nurses, and most people are unaware that the average nurse makes less than the average garbage collector. Nurses were also silent. More occupied with caring for their patients than with joining political movements, they rarely discussed inequities.

But no more. Increasingly today, nurses are speaking out about being browbeaten and intimidated by those physicians and healthcare executives who treat them more like robots than like educated professionals. And though this state of things is most certainly not a universal reality, healthcare executives are nonetheless understandably concerned about the new militancy and anger among nurses. The formation of unions could generate demand for higher pay and better benefits, which would, in turn, reinforce pressures to contain costs.

What's the solution? In the years ahead, healthcare executives may need to look at nurses from the patient's point of view. Think about it: During an average hospital stay, a patient sees more nurses than physicians. Nurses are on duty twenty-four hours, and the patient learns to depend on them for basic care and personal needs. Most attitudes about healthcare organizations are determined, not by the food, interior design, or the quality of the television picture, but by the way patients, visitors, and family members are treated by nurses.

Because nurses provide more hands-on care than anyone on the healthcare team, they manage hundreds of "moments of truth" that help people evaluate a healthcare organization.

In recent years, hospitals, nursing homes, and other healthcare institutions have started to recruit nurses in England, Scotland, Ireland, and other European countries. Although this is a useful emergency measure, much can be done within the United States.

If all healthcare executives offered their nurses equitable compensation packages, authentic opportunities for advancement, and opportunities to participate in the patient-care process, undoubtedly much of the distress and unrest would dissipate.

Nurses have always offered tender loving care, hope, and encouragement to their patients. It's time that healthcare executives uniformly offered the same to nurses.

34

Break down the barriers to delivering good service

How would you like to throw a pie in the face of a manager or senior executive and get away with it? The most successful service companies in America not only tolerate these antics—they encourage them.

One such company is Lenscrafters, which created a chain of stores where customers are examined and fitted for eyeglasses in one hour. In business since 1983, Lenscrafters has more than 275 stores in forty states. In 1987, they ranked fourth in number of stores within the optical industry, but they ranked second in sales. Given the company's current rate of growth, it should soon lead the industry in sales.

But why has Lenscrafters experienced such dramatic success? The answer is simple: The company focuses on quality and requires that all management personnel attend Precision Lenscrafters University. To ensure that Lenscrafters customers understand the company's dedication to quality, each store has a laboratory where customers can watch their glasses being made. In addition, everyone who works at Lenscrafters is called an associate—a practice patterned after the J.C. Penney Company.

One winter day when the wind chill in Davenport, Iowa, was minus 25, Lenscrafters employees Holly Stewart and Cheryl Vesco helped a woman select and fit a new pair of glasses in her car. The woman had broken both of her legs in an accident, and, because of the cold weather, she was unable to enter the store in her wheelchair. Then there's Cheryl Simpson, a Lenscrafters optician from Fort Worth, Texas, who joined her church group to do free vision screening on a Navajo Indian reservation in Arizona.

Much of the credit goes to Lenscrafters' superlative senior management. CEO Ban Hudson deserves a standing ovation for treating customers and associates with courtesy and respect. Hudson is a smart and creative businessman who understands that the essence of success is in helping people feel good about themselves and the people they serve. At Lenscrafters, the job of creating a strong and growing company is never really over.

One day, senior executives halted operations to give associates time to work on a list of the company's core values. The associates developed the following list:

✦ Nurture individuals.

✦ Build on people's strengths.

✦ Accept mistakes.

✦ Focus on winning, not on individual scoring.

✦ Push ideas.

✦ Make each store a separate business.

✦ Plan for the twenty-first century.

✦ Demand the highest quality.

✦ Constantly improve.

✦ Have fun.

One issue of *Eyewitness 2000*, Lenscrafters' company publication, features a story about an apprentice optician who won the contest for "most sales" in her store and who celebrated by throwing a pie at the store manager. Unfortunately, too many executives forget that humor and a sense of fun can make an incredible difference in the workplace.

35

Treat both your employees and your customers well

Roy Dement should be installed in the Service Employee Hall of Fame. The nomination is based on the ingenuity, initiative, and common sense displayed by Dement as a doorman at Toronto's Four Seasons Hotel.

One day, Dement neglected to load a departing guest's briefcase into his airport-bound taxi. Upon discovering his error, Dement immediately called the guest, who was a lawyer in Washington, D.C. When Dement learned that the guest needed the briefcase for a morning meeting, he did what any self-respecting employee of a five-star hotel would do—he got on a plane bound for Washington, D.C., and personally delivered the briefcase to the guest.

The Four Seasons recognized Dement's initiative and follow-through by making him employee of the year. The reasoning was simple: Four Seasons Hotels are dedicated to creating satisfied customers, and Dement had done his part to achieve that mission.

Chairman Isadore Sharp knows that the key to beating the occupancy and repeat business rates of competitors is to always be on the lookout for new ways "to get customers to love you."

Companies who treat their customers well also treat their employees well. "Some companies make the mistake of telling employees what to do to get close to the customer," said John Cunningham, president of a national training firm. "Good external service requires good internal service."

In summary, an organization can never expect its employees to treat customers well if the employees aren't treated the same way.

Isadore Sharp has internalized this lesson. He invests a significant portion of his time talking with housekeepers and concierges about their jobs. Like nurses and orderlies in the healthcare environment, these service professionals have the greatest contact with guests and contribute to fast and efficient service.

Is Isadore Sharp alone in his willingness to interact with the "little people" who help his organization to prosper year after year? He probably has compatriots in many industries. But how many chief executive officers in the healthcare industry take time to visit with food service workers, laboratory technicians, or admitting representatives? How many times are dedicated, hard-working service professionals queried about how they feel and what they do?

Smart healthcare executives should treat employees well if for no other reason than that these employees will then in turn extend the same kindness and concern to patients, visitors, and families.

Treating your customers well is essential, but that won't happen unless your employees first feel good about themselves and what they do. The Four Seasons' treatment of Roy Dement is a classic example.

36

Investing in human capital

You know, we've been slower than some industries in investing in *human capital*. Somehow, we thought those nurses and therapists would always be around when we wanted them.

But now we're facing serious shortages of therapists, pharmacists, and certain product-line managers. And how do you recruit and retain these people in an era of possible downsizing or resizing?

A lot of these people will be able to pick and choose where they work, and like most of us, they'll only work for organizations that treat them like valued professionals and worthwhile human beings. And you can't blame them—you'd want the same things too.

What we now have to realize is that we're not going to be dealing with the same kinds of people who came to us—hat in hand—ten, fifteen, or twenty years ago—people who were grateful for the chance to collect a paycheck. Experts vary on this, but personally, I think what we have out there—for better or for worse—is a new breed of worker.

In his new book *Why Work: Leading the New Generation*, Michael Maccoby, who also wrote a pretty famous book called *The Gamesman*, writes about the new breed of workers called self-developers. Here's a profile of them:

✦ They want to be business people, not bureaucrats.

✦ They search for meaning beyond success, or for success beyond money and status.

✦ They say that work shouldn't be the most important thing in life.

✦ They want to learn from models, not copy them.

Now, does that sound like some of the younger staff or management people in your organization? Well, not everyone fits the profile, but one thing is sure: People expect more from the workplace than just a paycheck—and whether you're talking about occupational therapists or food service workers, the future belongs to the organization that treats its employees as associates and valued customers.

How do we find and develop workers who want more than a 9-to-5 routine but who will still be committed to the organization? In the 1990s, that's going to be one of our biggest challenges!

37

King Customer

n bold letters on the cover of *Business Week* were two words:
King Customer. As I read the cover article, I began to
ruminate about how customers are generally treated by
most businesses—at best indifferently and at worst badly.

It's hard to believe that such an attitude exists in this day
and age, but it does. Too many people think of customers as
an imposition on their time and a drain on their energies.
They take customers for granted, when any encounter with
one should be considered valuable, because customers are the
lifeblood of any business.

I think too many businesses want to blame foreign competition, or the failure of a certain market to develop, or anything
else for their failures, instead of blaming themselves for not
paying more attention to their customers. But that's not
surprising, because many top executives are so far removed
from what is going on in the trenches that the customer is
thought of as an impersonal statistic rather than as an individual with feelings, who craves to be treated with dignity and
respect.

According to *Business Week*, the companies that fawn over
their customers in the 1990s will be successful. Let me cite an
example from the article. In the early 1980s, most people who
flew on British Airways referred to the airline as "bloody
awful." Service was poor, personnel were gruff and rude, and
customers were treated as though everything would be just
great if they simply disappeared.

But in 1983, Colin Marshall took over as chief executive

officer, and that's when things began to change. Right off the bat, Mr. Marshall went to his customers for help and asked them what they expected from his airline.

Their responses seemed quite logical to those of us who travel all the time. What they overwhelmingly asked for was to be treated well by the British Airways staff. After that earth-shaking revelation, Liam Strong, BA's marketing director, is quoted as saying: "We decided service excellence, not operations, was going to drive the business."

Then Mr. Marshall and other BA executives traveled all over the world telling all 35,000 employees what their new objective was, and making sure that every employee realized that without his or her dedication, caring, and participation, the airline wasn't going to succeed.

It took months, but it must have worked, because for the fiscal year ending March 31, 1989, BA had sales of $8.2 billion, with pretax profits up about 19 percent to $544 million. Not bad for an airline that just a few years ago was considered one of the worst anywhere.

Opportunity. There's plenty of it, because many companies still don't get the point. Whether it's publishing or healthcare or computers, taking care of customers is going to be the success blueprint for the '90s. Not the shallow, lip-service type of commitment that many companies make, but a deep and costly commitment to make sure customers are treated right.

Of course, that's one of the problems with customer service. It costs money. More money than many companies want to spend, because in the short term it negatively affects the bottom line. But those organizations that really care will spend the money, because they know that in the long term the customer is truly king.

If you aren't continually preoccupied with the needs of your customers, I suggest you get off the playing field, because you won't even have a chance of surviving, much less winning. The customer is definitely king.

38

The high cost
of substandard service

One of the biggest and most valid complaints against advertising is that it promises more than it can realistically deliver. The potential customer is misled and quickly becomes disgruntled and disillusioned.

This scenario is being repeated in the healthcare industry. Providers have invested huge sums of money in image advertising and in advertising to sell specific products and services. But can these organizations deliver on their promises?

The answer would appear to be yes and no. All too often, people complain about shabby personal treatment in the hospital setting. In every case, they express anger, resentment, and disappointment about the behavior of technicians, nurses, physicians, or management staff.

With the industry-wide rush toward guest relations and quality management, the perception is that hospital patients are being treated as valued customers.

But the reality is that patients seem to complain less about runaway prices than about indifference, arrogance, and a laissez-faire attitude on the part of caregivers and service personnel.

Some healthcare providers have a defense. As one nurse said to a patient, "We're not running a hotel here, and this isn't room service."

Unfortunately, organizations pay a price for these attitudes. Patients, family members, and visitors who go away with negative attitudes talk to friends and neighbors. Before long, a hospital ends up with a less than stellar reputation—not because the quality of medical care is inferior, but because service is substandard.

39

Build a service culture

In their book *Service America*, Karl Albrecht and Ron Zemke chronicle the opportunities that exist for companies that want to make service a top organizational priority. Their formula: Make a total commitment to service.

To do so, people who run the company must set an example and provide an environment where each employee understands his or her role in the total scheme of business. Building a service culture takes time, training, and discipline, but most important, it takes leaders who are committed to excellence, care about their customers, and are willing to take risks to bring about change.

Think about it. Our economy is organized around service, but most of the service we receive as clients, consumers, and customers is below par. How many times have you heard a vendor or retailer joke, "If it weren't for customers, I'd really enjoy my job"?

Healthcare is a service business, but I wonder how many providers really understand and internalize that message? One hospital executive was truthful enough to confide in me that he often marveled at how much hospital patients would tolerate.

But providers aren't alone. Many vendors and consultants have yet to wake up to the fact that providing excellent service is an integral component of success. Many providers tell horror stories about getting service on equipment for which they had just paid thousands of dollars.

And consider just what poor service can cost a company.

According to one study, 25 percent of an organization's clients are upset enough to cease doing business with the company. And only 4 percent of these customers ever bother to voice their complaint. The remaining 96 percent simply prefer to switch rather than fight.

Maintaining customer loyalty is the best argument for staying in touch with your customers. Stay involved, and know what they're thinking and feeling. In the end, a commitment to understanding the people you serve means far more than a few well-chosen words in an expensive brochure.

40

Smart like a fox

Ole Olson and his wife, Darlene, run the Main Street Restaurant in Detroit Lakes, Minnesota—a small town about forty miles east of Fargo, North Dakota.

I know the Main Street Restaurant, because I have a cottage near there, and each summer my wife and I spend a few weeks enjoying the fresh air and the country hospitality.

Now, to my way of thinking, Ole Olson and his wife are something special. I just wish that anyone who's in a service business could watch Ole, his wife, and all the cooks and waitresses at the Main Street Restaurant in action. Let me explain.

Traveling all over the country on business, I've eaten in some pretty fancy places. You know, the kind where, when you get the bill, you flinch, knowing that what you've spent on one night's dinner could feed some families for a month. Mentally, I think I'll always have trouble with that. And the maitre d's and waiters and waitresses are all nice enough, but too often I don't think they really care about their customers.

But that's not the case at Ole Olson's Main Street Restaurant. As soon as you enter, you know somebody really does care. And you're always greeted with a smile by Ole, who makes you feel special and wanted—something rare in this day and age.

And then there's the food. Like the breakfast special for $2.10 that includes two eggs, bacon, and pancakes. Lunches and dinners are equally reasonably priced—and delicious. And the food is always presented by smiling waitresses, who always come back to make sure everything is all right. In between, there's Ole, smiling and laughing and greeting people. If there's a line waiting, he makes sure everyone has a cup of coffee. His enthusiasm and caring are contagious. The restaurant literally reeks with conviviality.

One morning, I asked Ole about his philosophy of doing business, and this is what he told me: "Good service, quality food, reasonably priced."

On people: "There's got to be teamwork, and I've got to set the example. If people aren't happy, they won't help my customers, so I've got to make sure they are happy."

And then he talks about customers. "We are here so short a time, and my wife and I think people are beautiful. Many of our customers are senior citizens, and they eat all three meals here. They keep coming back, and that makes us feel good."

So that's the story of Ole Olson, his wife, Darlene, and their son, Eric, who helps out in the summers when he's home from college, running the Main Street Restaurant in a small town in Minnesota.

Some big-time operators might scoff at the likes of Ole Olson—even call him bush league. But in my opinion, Ole Olson is big league in every way. And I think a lot of companies would do well to follow his philosophy of taking care of customers.

Surprising how smart these country people are. Just like a fox.

41

"Kill 'em with kindness"

In 1987, *Fortune* magazine published an article entitled "America's Best Salesmen." Those profiled were not corporate moguls or high rollers, but well-meaning, average Americans who sold shoes, vacuum cleaners, cars, computers, real estate, boats, and stocks.

Although their backgrounds varied, all were successful in the selling profession. Moreover, they shared in common one attribute: an overwhelming sense of concern for meeting their customers' needs.

Unfortunately, too many salespeople are so concerned with their own needs that they forget that their mission is to take care of customers. For some, catering to the whims of customers is demeaning and demoralizing. For others, preoccupation with commissions and quick results makes them neglect long-term relationships.

Cecile Satterwhite sells women's shoes at Leon's in Tyler, Texas. Because she sells about $600,000 to $700,000 worth of shoes annually, she makes a salary of about $100,000. But for Cecile, selling shoes is a labor of love. On any given day, six or seven women will be lined up waiting for the opportunity to buy shoes from Cecile.

And what's the secret of her success? "I love to sell," she says. "It's exciting, and it gets into your blood." Cecile is so thrilled with the business of selling shoes that she typically doesn't leave the store for lunch and gets nervous on Sundays when Leon's is closed.

Asked why women come from all over the state of Texas to

buy from her, Cecile replied, "We just kill 'em with kindness."

Selling is a profession, but for those individuals who fall in love with the experience, it becomes an art form and a way of life. Selling reaches its heights when it's practiced by people like Cecile Satterwhite. She not only likes to make money, but also thrills at the opportunity to cater to the whims of her customers.

People like Cecile Satterwhite don't always walk in the door wearing Brooks Brothers suits or carrying an Ivy League M.B.A., but they're almost always worth a long and aggressive search.

Healthcare organizations, consulting firms, and vendors who fail to seek out strong salespeople are only postponing the inevitable. Although sophisticated executive search firms can shoulder part of the burden, the organization's management must be involved in the search process.

But your job isn't over when the salesperson signs on the dotted line. You need to give them the environment and encouragement they need to help you knock the socks off your competitors.

42

Make the customer your reason for existence

Not long ago I was waiting to see the marketing manager of American Laundry Company. On the wall was a sign that appears in many laundry and dry cleaning establishments—as well as other businesses—across the nation. Simple, concrete, and direct, it listed the following Ten Commandments of Good Business:

✦ A CUSTOMER is the most important person in any business.

✦ A CUSTOMER is not dependent on us—we are dependent on him.

✦ A CUSTOMER is not an interruption of our work—he is the purpose of it.

✦ A CUSTOMER does us a favor when he calls—we are not doing him a favor by serving him.

✦ A CUSTOMER is a part of our business—not an outsider.

✦ A CUSTOMER is not a cold statistic—he is a flesh-and-blood human being with feelings like our own.

✦ A CUSTOMER is not someone to argue or match wits with.

✦ A CUSTOMER is a person who brings us his wants—it is our job to fulfill those wants.

✦ A CUSTOMER is deserving of the most courteous and

attentive treatment we can give him.

✦ A CUSTOMER is the lifeblood of this and every other business.

No matter what your profession or industry, these ten commandments say it all. If you deal with clients and customers and pursue your craft without these commandments in the back of your mind, your success will probably be short- lived.

On the other hand, people who continually consider customers' needs will probably come out winners. Healthcare executives have one major complaint about vendors and consultants: Although they receive promises of good service, the service that's delivered usually falls short of expectations.

In this age of mergers, takeovers, alliances, and elaborate competitive strategies, the most important person in the equation—the customer—is often minimized or overlooked. Whether you sell high-tech equipment, women's healthcare, or membership programs for the elderly, taking care of the customer will always be the centerpiece of effective sales and marketing.

Keeping your word, following up, and rendering good service will never go out of style.

43

Learn the nitty-gritty aspects of rendering service

I f you want to be inspired by customer service and success, there's nothing better than examining case examples on how to do it.

Riverside Methodist Hospital is the flagship institution of U.S. Healthcare, Columbus, Ohio. Eric Chapman III, Riverside's chief executive officer, understands operations from the inside out, because he often leaves his business suit in his office and works alongside crews in the laundry, kitchen, or in radiology. He's even served as a patient escort and pushed patients in wheelchairs.

Part of Chapman's success is due to his self-concept. He views himself as a change agent within the American health-care system and believes there are far too many similarities between what goes on in the healthcare system and in the prison system. Many people who visit or are admitted to a hospital do so reluctantly.

And why wouldn't they? One of the first indignities patients experience is wearing a "degrading uniform commonly referred to as a patient gown."

A similar approach to that of Riverside Methodist is seen at Boston's Beth Israel Hospital, where admitted patients receive a primary care nurse who has twenty-four-hour responsibility for the patient's daily nursing care. In other words, the nurse is totally involved in everything that happens to his or her patient/customer.

The Mayo Clinic's international reputation for service results in 80 percent of patients coming in on their own. And no one mentions payment until after treatment is completed. Insurance forms are filled out when you leave, not when you arrive.

The experiences of Riverside, Beth Israel, and Mayo remind us of the centrality of service within healthcare, and that unless we provide good service, we won't be in business very long.

44

Totally committed to customer service

Being treated rudely sends me up the wall, puts me in a bad mood, and makes me surly. Ever said "Good morning" to someone and had them completely ignore you? It doesn't sit well. Or how about phoning a company and being treated with indifference by the person answering?

More often than not, your first reaction to rude treatment is to be rude in return. At least, that's the way I've always felt. Now there's a study to support this contention. Professor Joseph Weintraub at Babson College near Boston conducted a study to find out how people felt when they were treated both well and badly.

Many interesting things came from the study, which should be must reading for anyone interested in customer service or sales, or just with dealing with people on a day-to-day basis.

One thing Weintraub found was that 71 percent of the individuals surveyed said they would take their business elsewhere if they were treated rudely, even if it meant higher prices. Only 36 percent said they would shop at a store that was convenient but had poor customer service.

Weintraub, who also runs a business called Organizational Dimensions, claims that the keys to good customer service include customer-service training and top management commitment to good service. To this he adds something that I personally believe makes all the difference in the world. He says, "You need to find and hire people who have values consistent with your organization's customer orientation. Organizations have to make it clear that good service is rewarded."

Now, Weintraub's research hasn't discovered anything that previous management gurus haven't told us before. People like to be treated with dignity and respect, and if they are, they'll practically break down the door to do business with you.

I can recall going into inconveniently located stores, whose prices weren't particularly reasonable, and finding them loaded with customers. The answer is simple and obvious. The salespeople are very attentive, have smiles on their faces, and make sure that all the customers are being taken care of.

Another thing: Whenever I witness good retail service, I notice that the boss is visible. He or she is in the midst of the action, not hidden in some office or ivory tower. And that's another part of good service: management's involvement. It's critical, whether in retail, medical supplies, or the hospital business. In fact, some of the best healthcare executives in the business actually go from patient room to patient room, making sure everything is all right.

Good people are the key to good service. And haven't you noticed that quality people attract other quality people? Also, people have to be trained and updated on a regular basis. Individuals left unattended fall into bad habits.

Too many healthcare institutions think they are different from other businesses when it comes to customer service. And that includes their physician customers as well as their patients. But I keep telling them that they are not different. They must stay on top of customer service and be totally committed to the concept. Hiring good people, training them properly, and then rewarding them with money or vacations—or both—is becoming more commonplace in the healthcare industry, and it's a good trend.

Any healthcare institution that hopes to be around in the year 2000 had better get on the bandwagon. It's simply good common sense.

45

The moment of truth

Back in 1987, I took a Piedmont flight from Lexington, Kentucky, to Chicago. Because I had a head cold and ear congestion, I knew that the descent into O'Hare Airport might be painful.

I jokingly shared my concern with the co-pilot, who, to my surprise, said, "I'm glad you told me, because I'll make sure we don't descend too quickly when we land in Chicago."

At first, I thought he was just trying to make me feel better, but by the time we hit the runway at O'Hare, I realized that the descent had indeed been gradual. And as I left the aircraft, the co-pilot asked me if I was OK.

What I had experienced on that Piedmont flight was what service experts Ron Zemke and Karl Albrecht call a "moment of truth." Every organization—no matter what the industry—has positive and negative "moments of truth."

Someone might call a trade association or professional society with a simple question and receive a rude, abrupt, or confusing answer. According to Zemke, Albrecht, and other service experts, a person's perception of an organization will depend on the quality of communication with the first contact.

Examples of such moments of truth exist in every area of life. How many times have you gone into a retail store and had to beg for service from a lackadaisical or indifferent sales-clerk? Or how many times have you been in an emergency room and waited hours for service?

An executive vice president of a Fortune 500 company

injured his ankle while playing tennis one morning and decided to visit the emergency room of the hospital where he was a trustee.

He limped in, identified himself, showed his insurance card, filled out some forms, and was told to sit down. After two hours of waiting, he decided that his ankle felt better, and he left. For him, that had been a definitive moment of truth.

These moments of truth have one feature in common: They rarely concern the quality of the product or service. Instead, they usually involve communication, courtesy, and follow-up.

Although Piedmont Aviation was merged with USAir in August 1989, I have positive memories of a co-pilot who, late one night on a flight to Chicago, took time to make me feel more like a person than a passenger.

Meeting Personal Challenges

*I've learned that all high achievers share these
characteristics in common: a passion for
success—and a passion for living.*

46

Develop a positive, winning attitude

In 1987, a barge of garbage floated aimlessly off our nation's coasts. The U.S. Conference of Mayors predicted that by the late 1990s, landfill capacity in more than half of our cities would be exhausted.

In the midst of this crisis, an entrepreneur named David Baker maintained that garbage could be turned into oil through a process called pyrolysis. The most telling observation about this breakthrough thinker came from the *Chicago Tribune.*

"People like Dave Baker always seem to appear at times like this, undaunted by what others see as impending disaster," the *Tribune* wrote. "To him this is an opportunity. Given lemons, he'll make lemonade."

Has our nation successfully turned garbage into oil? Not exactly. But my industry—healthcare—is full of wonderful, crazy people like Dave Baker who refuse to believe predictions of doom and who manage to turn their organizations around.

In the same way, the vendors and consulting firms to my industry have done cartwheels to help their clients survive and prosper. New products and pharmaceuticals are continually being developed to help healthcare professionals save hundreds of thousands of lives.

These people can take the most demoralizing circumstances and turn them into new opportunities. They have the kind of positive, winning attitude that's absolutely essential in today's healthcare environment—as well as in life. The battle cry of my industry—and yours—can no longer be, "Isn't it awful?" Like Dave Baker, we need to stare adversity in the face and proclaim, "What an opportunity!"

47

Laugh and the world laughs with you

Having a sense of humor is one of the most important attributes you can develop—in business and in life. The healthcare industry has just begun to discover the therapeutic benefits of humor, and many healthcare organizations have introduced innovative programs into the hospital's routine offerings.

Kathy Knight, a nurse in Albuquerque, New Mexico, founded a group called Humor and Hospitals Are Healthy Allies, better known as HAHAHA. Pictured on a poster touting the organization is Ina Carlson, a woman who has had two heart attacks and quadruple bypass surgery. Her explanation for laughter in the face of her setbacks is simple: "Why not? That's what keeps me going. Wouldn't it be awful if I sat back and cried?"

"Research findings are beginning to accumulate that suggest that laughter may be therapeutic and could be used to reduce disease symptoms," according to Lars Ljungdahl of the Lyckorna Primary Health Care Center in Motala, Sweden.

And Lee Berk, M.D., of the School of Medicine at Loma Linda University in Loma Linda, California, agrees: "Laughter indeed may be like a good medicine."

He cites a study in which ten people watched a humorous video for two hours and had blood samples taken every ten minutes. The effect was a healthy drop in blood pressure, heart rate, and hormones that are released during stress.

But humor may not be alone in its power to heal. Joseph Neumann, a psychologist with the Veterans Administration in Johnson City, Tennessee, believes that humor is therapeutic, but probably no better than other activities that induce pleasure—such as relaxing music.

In a study of two groups of patients who experienced surgery under a local anesthetic, he found no difference between those who listened to an old Jack Benny radio show and those who listened to soothing ocean sounds.

Back at University Hospital in Albuquerque, Kathy Knight and her team continue to spread humor with wall posters and special carts loaded with everything from balloons and bubbles to comic books and videos.

Think of it. In the twenty-first century, physicians may be judged by their one-liners as much as by their surgical skills!

So if you happen to be walking down a hospital corridor anytime soon, don't be surprised if you hear a nurse, physician, or even an executive, begin a conversation with, "Have you heard the one about . . . ?"

It's their way of helping patients feel better and heal more quickly, and fortunately, it seems to be working.

48

No matter what
happens, keep moving

Back in the late 1940s and 1950s, the big bands of Stan
Kenton, Count Basie, Harry James, Woody Herman,
Tommy and Jimmy Dorsey, and others played the
sounds that people my age listened and danced to.

Many of those big-band leaders are dead now, but one
musician who looked like he just might go on forever was
Woody Herman. At age 72, Woody played an average of
twenty-seven halls and ballrooms in as many cities each
month. And that was month after month, year after year.

What was amazing about Woody Herman was that his
personal problems would have sent lesser people into therapy
or jail—or both. In 1985, the IRS almost auctioned off his
Hollywood Hills home to satisfy back taxes he owed. Fortunately, show business friends such as Frank Sinatra, Tony
Bennett, and Peggy Lee offered to pay his rent and other
expenses. As of 1986, he still owed the government $1.6
million—the result of trusting his finances to a manager for
whom gambling became a disease.

But in the midst of these crises, Woody Herman still played
his share of benefit concerts. What made this elderly musician
such an inspiration? His schedule made that of the average
business executive look like a vacation, and he was overrun
with personal financial problems.

But in the face of it all, Woody refused to blame anyone
for the tough hand he was forced to play. He just kept doing

what he loved most: playing his clarinet.

In October 1987, Woody Herman died at the age of 74. In an obituary, *Chicago Tribune* correspondent Larry Kart quoted Woody Herman's perspective on life: "Leading big bands is my hobby—a hobby I happen to believe in," he said.

In an episode of "60 Minutes," Count Basie was asked: "Count, don't you get sick of all this travel and one-night stands? Doesn't it ever wear on you?"

The Count replied in a style reminiscent of Woody Herman. "Look, this is my life," he said. "I love it, and if I didn't, I'd get out of it."

When I hear people complain about how work interferes with the real business of life or that they can hardly wait for their next vacation, I wonder why they can't transfer equal amounts of enthusiasm to their jobs.

Fortunately, there are other people who can't wait to share a recent business success and who look forward to every working day. They approach their work life with zest and spark, and if they haven't already achieved success, they soon will. You'll never catch them counting the days until Friday or Christmas vacation, because they're involved and intrigued with what they do.

Having work that you enjoy is a blessing. It's no wonder that Woody Herman and Count Basie dominated the big-band scene for so many years. They loved their work, and they weren't afraid to talk about it.

So the next time you feel put upon by a canceled flight or tight meeting schedule, think of Woody Herman and Count Basie and their abiding love for big-band jazz. Then you'll remember how lucky you really are!

49

Enthusiasm, dreams, hard work, and heart

In the mid-1980s, a friend of mine started his own consulting business. The first two years were touch and go, but within five years, he had five consultants working for him. How does he see his business? "We show hospitals how to manage change," he said—and by the look of things, the 1990s should deliver plenty of business opportunities for his firm.

Here are his personal secrets for success: First, be enthusiastic. Without enthusiasm and a zest for work and for life, no one can go very far. If you don't believe it, think of how much fun you have around enthusiastic people. They make even dead-end situations bearable, because one of their most basic aims in life is to have fun and share their joy with others.

Next, dream your dreams, and make them come true. Allow yourself the luxury and pleasure of dreaming. If you cut short your dreams, you'll be missing out on one of life's greatest pleasures.

How often we have heard people confide, "I dreamed of this happening, and now it's come true," or "I spent years fantasizing about being here, and now it's really happened." In most cases, giving yourself permission to dream is the first step in making your dreams come true.

Third, work hard, and do more than pay lip service to the work ethic. People who succeed are devoted to the work ethic. They don't need coddling, pampering, inspiring, or prodding. As the popular commercial for a sportswear manufacturer claims, they "just do it." Work, perseverance, and follow-through are integral to their personality and sense of self. The best athletes, healthcare executives, journalists, and economists may vary in talent, skill, experience, and ideology, but they share one thing in common: All have a strong work ethic.

Finally, take heart. Enthusiasm, dreams, and a strong work ethic are a powerful combination, but they're nothing without the kicker that comes with heart.

Heart means keeping your own counsel. Heart means continuing to try—even after everyone else has surrendered. Heart means playing by the rules and sticking to your principles. Heart means playing it straight with your colleagues and friends. And heart means the courage to be gentle, sensitive, and vulnerable, and if necessary, even to play the fool.

These are deceptively simple concepts. But perhaps that's another critical lesson: Stick to the basics, and keep your life very simple.

50

Go the distance

In October 1989, the life of Kenneth Jennings changed forever. Trying to make a tackle on the opening kickoff of a high school football game, he broke his neck. Unable to move his head, and with only limited use of his upper shoulder muscles, he may be a quadriplegic for the remainder of his life.

Kenneth Jennings is no newcomer to disappointment. Raised without a father, he is the fourth of five children and spent most of his childhood in a housing project on Chicago's South Side. His youngest brother is autistic; his niece has spina bifida; and just a few years ago, he helped his mother battle breast cancer.

And yet, in the face of incredible adversity, Kenneth Jennings is always photographed with a smiling face. It is the smile of love, of hope, of youth, and of a winner. Part of the credit may go to the Rehabilitation Institute of Chicago, where Kenneth Jennings received the care and treatment that was so critical to his recovery and eventual return to high school.

Immediately after the accident, most of the physicians who examined Kenneth were convinced he would never breathe without the aid of a machine. But in December 1988, he started breathing on his own, and in May 1989, he returned to high school as a full-time student.

Even walking is not outside his vision. "I feel there's always a possibility that I'll walk again," he says. "I believe it will happen. I don't know when. But I'm not going to stop my life then quitting your job because you think you're going to win. Then, when you don't win, you're left with nothing."

Kenneth Jennings will probably beat the odds and walk again, because he refuses to surrender to physicians' verdicts and predictions about his fate. Rather than drowning in self-pity, he elects to look on the brighter side of life. Although he's confined to a 200-pound wheelchair, Kenneth Jennings will move and make things happen. He already has.

The world is full of people like Kenneth Jennings who joyfully cope with adversity and overcome impossible odds simply because they're thankful to be alive. This is the legacy of people like Kenneth Jennings.

No matter what happens, never allow self-pity to be the victor. Instead, challenge and confront life, and know that promise and opportunity are everywhere.

51

Accept responsibility for your actions

Pick up any newspaper or magazine, and you read about people who consistently blame a system, culture, political party, or race for what's happened to them. Some even go so far as to instigate legal action and win settlements for hundreds of thousands of dollars.

These people may succeed in taking some of the wear and tear out of daily life, but their rush to blame others for personal mistakes and failures is a sad commentary on modern life. How often do we hear people blame their spouse for their own drinking? And how many times do we hear people blame smoking on the pressures of their jobs? And then there's the athlete who claims that he can't score because of an unfair umpire or referee.

Fortunately, there are other people who have the courage to admit their failures. When you hear such comments as "Boy, did I goof up," "That was my fault," or "Don't worry, I can fix it," you're dealing with a special kind of person.

But why this epidemic of blaming others for personal mistakes and inadequacies? The answer is that it's easy. The simplest way to explain failure is to avoid responsibility and blame circumstances or another person.

One key trait that separates successful people from others is an ability to accept responsibility for their actions and accomplishments. Listen to successful people reflect on the downside of life, and you'll hear them say, "I got beaten out that time, but I'm going to make it happen the next time around," or "I didn't perform the way I could have, but this is a learning experience, and I'll do better next time." When you hear remarks such as these from a business executive or salesperson, it's usually from top performers. If you hear such comments as "They didn't like me," "Nobody told me to call on that person," or "I sent them the information, but they didn't read it," you're probably talking to people who've lost their ability to be honest and objective.

Losers are notorious for rationalizing their behavior and wallowing in self-pity. Winners, by contrast, tell it exactly like it is—the good and bad.

52

Helping others is its own reward

I n the summer of 1989, I was driving back from my summer cabin in Minnesota with my three dogs. Despite the intense heat, I had planned to make it to Chicago in twelve hours.

About nine hours into the trip, I pulled into a rest area outside of Madison, Wisconsin. And then it happened. In a rush, I grabbed one of my dogs, flipped the master door switch, got out of the car, and slammed the door. In doing so, I had locked myself out of the car with the motor running and the air conditioning blasting away. I didn't have an extra set of keys, and for a few minutes, I had visions of the car overheating, catching fire, and blowing up—with my other two dogs inside.

I shared my plight with two young men, who suggested that I call the state police. The police said they would send a locksmith, but they couldn't tell me when.

Then a short, burly, unshaven man approached me. He had been listening to my troubles, and he thought he might be able to help. You see, at one time he had been an auto body man, and he knew he could work magic with a wire coat hanger.

Five minutes later, my car was unlocked, and my dogs made a break for freedom. Then the auto body man started to share his own tale of woe. Earlier that day he had lost an address book that contained all of his business and personal phone numbers, and now, his truck was overheated. But he said with a smile, "That's the way things go every once in a while."

When I tried to give him ten dollars, he stopped and said, "You know, if I take your money, it really takes away the meaning of what I just did. Just remember that all truck drivers aren't bad."

That trucker had just gone through one of the tougher days of his life, but he still took time to help someone out of a fix. Although he was scheduled to have his load in Indianapolis by 3:00 P.M., it was already after three o'clock when he came to my aid at a Wisconsin rest stop. I know very little about that trucker except that his name is Charlie, and I'll never forget his kindness.

Fortunately, the highways are full of people like Charlie. If you ever have the good fortune to meet them, do what I did: Let their employers know that it's great to have them on the open road.

53

Give freely to others

D ick Hodgins and I became close buddies when we were stationed at Osaka Army General Hospital in Japan. Young and far away from home, we carried on some heavy discussions about life and the world.

It was Christmas Eve 1954 when Dick turned to me and said, "Christmas is great, but I wish people would care about each other every day the way they do during the Christmas holidays."

Decades have passed since that Christmas Eve far away from home, but Dick's wise words still ring in my ears. Today's newspapers are peppered with stories, not of the Korean conflict, but of a basketball giant named Michael Jordan. As a professional basketball player, he has no equal. During the 1988 NBA playoffs, he took a mediocre team to the finals and scored an average of 40-50 points per game.

No one would mistake Dick Hodgins for Michael Jordan on the street, but they share a wonderful spirit. On people who are down on their luck, Jordan said, "That's often the way it is, I guess. The people who need it are too proud to ask. That's why it's up to us who have something to spread it around."

And on giving panhandlers money, he said, "I was just walking up the street, and a man came up to me and asked me for some dough so he could eat. I didn't have a five- or ten-dollar bill, so I have him a hundred. I don't know how it made him feel when I gave him the money, but I know how it made me feel. How can anyone experience the warm feeling you get inside when you give something to somebody and not want to do it again and again?"

On handicapped kids, when he gave of his time and talent to the Special Olympics: "I was a little scared at first. I mean, some of them can't walk like we walk and can't talk like we talk. But then you realize they can't hate like we hate and deceive like we deceive, or cheat like we cheat. They only know how to love and trust. People like me have been so lucky, and yet that's the one place I can go where everyone is so sincere."

Fortunately, opportunities to put Michael Jordan's advice into practice are never in short supply. At a local restaurant, I once saw a young mother eating dinner with her two kids and their father, and as I watched them, it became obvious that eating out was a special experience. So when the waiter brought me my check, I asked if I could pick up their check as well. It was only twenty dollars, but when I left that restaurant, I felt as if I had won the lottery.

For a few moments, I became part of the legacy of everyday benefactors like Dick Hodgins and Michael Jordan. It made me wonder why Christmas comes only once a year.

54

Honor your father and mother

It's a terrible but inescapable tragedy to lose your mother or father. In 1989, two people who work for *Modern Healthcare* lost their parents. They worked hard to overcome their tragedy, but it wasn't easy for either of them. As the weeks and months passed, the pain and hurt became more muted and distant, but in some ways, I know that they'll never fully recover.

My mother was 28 years old when she died of tuberculosis. Although I was only 5 when it happened, I remember the day as if it were yesterday. I wasn't permitted to accompany my father to see her, so I sat downstairs in the sanitarium. I must have sensed something was wrong, because I cried until my father returned to pick me up.

Today, I have few visible memories of my mother—save a few photographs of her and some of the friends she had made at the sanitarium. And then there's the local newspaper announcement of her marriage to my father, Frederick Foulston Lauer. Her maiden name was Mildred Griffin, and to this day I often wonder what it would have been like to know her as I grew into a teenager, adult, and a father with children of my own.

In 1968, I lost my father to lung cancer. He rarely expressed his feelings, but I knew he was proud of me from the things he said and did. Many of his friends said he talked about me all the time. And whenever I fell on my face, he picked me up, salvaged my sagging self-confidence, and pushed me in the right direction.

Although I lived with my mother's parents in West Virginia, my father took me on business trips and introduced me to his clients. Often he would let me sit on his lap and steer the car. At other times, we would just sing songs together. On hot summer days we would lie down together on a hotel-room couch—a pitcher of ice water at our side—and listen to baseball games on the radio. Most of the time I would fall asleep.

There were fathers who were more successful or prominent, but I would never have traded mine for any of them. He believed in the spirit of America, and he believed in keeping his word. Despite his rough exterior, he believed in treating women with gentleness and a bit of chivalry. He believed in his company and his boss. But most important, he believed in people—especially the unassuming "little people" who rarely received the attention and respect they deserved.

Few words of comfort and concern can lessen the loss of a parent. Perhaps that's the greatest reason for honoring your mother and father while they still grace your life. And if you do lose your parents, be grateful for the memories they have given you.

Your mother and father will be with you forever, because they are part of you. In your darkest moments, when all seems lost, know that all they want from you is your best and happiness for the rest of your life. As I get older, I find myself thinking more about my mother and father. Although the pain of their loss is no longer as intense, I sometimes feel a twinge of sadness and regret.

So make sure your dreams come true—your mother and father would have wanted it that way. And you couldn't find a better way to pay tribute to their memory.

55

Live your life with style and grace

The last time I saw Fred Astaire was in 1975 at Chasen's Restaurant in Los Angeles. He was one of my idols, and seeing him in person was one of the biggest thrills of my life.

I tried to be casual about watching him, but I finally gave up the pretense. From time to time, I just stared at him as he lunched with his friends and greeted an endless stream of well-wishers. At the time, he was in his late seventies and still exhibited the charm, grace, and good humor that had brought him fame in films.

But there are many things about Fred Astaire that few people know. He knew how to handle rejection. Born Frederick Austerlitz in 1899 in Omaha, Nebraska, he was the son of a salesman. Like all good salesmen, he learned to cope with rejection. When he took his first screen test in the 1930s, a studio executive wrote: "No screen personality. Can't act. Can't sing. Balding. Dances a little."

Astaire had a sense of modesty and humor. When he was reminded of that early rejection later in his career, he was inclined to agree with the studio executive's assessment. "I never thought a funny-looking guy like me would be suitable for pictures."

Astaire could laugh at himself. He made the difficult look easy. He could make the most difficult dance moves look smooth and effortless. And what was his secret? "Practice, sweat, rehearsal, and worry," he replied. And most of us would agree. Few professionals perfect their craft without sweat, practice, and worry.

Astaire had charm. Charm and graciousness are often minimized or overlooked in the modern world. That's unfortunate, because people acquire these qualities over a period of years and through a variety of life experiences. Above all, charm means the willingness to engage, interact with, and listen to another person.

If Astaire had chosen to be a salesman, he probably would have been a good one. Fortunately, he chose to become an entertainer, and the world is a better and happier place because of his decision.

56

Never give up

In the late 1930s and 1940s, just about everyone knew of Glen Cunningham, one of the greatest runners this country has ever produced. In the 1936 Olympics, he won a silver medal in the 1500-meter race, and throughout the 1930s he set numerous records, highlighted by an outdoor mile of 4 minutes, 6.7 seconds in 1938.

In 1933, he won the Sullivan Award as America's top amateur athlete. He won the Wanamaker mile at New York's Millrose Games six times—more often than anyone else in history. Between 1933 and 1940, Glen Cunningham lost only once—when he was second in the Olympics.

Accolades continued—even to the present day. In 1979, he was named the best athlete in the 100-year history of Madison Square Garden, and in 1988—at age 78—he was brought back to run a leg in the commemorative event at the Millrose Games. Several weeks later, Glen Cunningham died on his farm in Conway, Arkansas.

The most astonishing feature in Glen Cunningham's life was not his awards, but what he had to endure to reach the pinnacle of athletic success. At the age of seven, he was severely burned in a school explosion and fire in Elkhart, Kansas. His brother was killed in that explosion, and Cunningham suffered burns so serious that physicians told his parents he might never walk again. But no medical diagnosis would deter young Cunningham.

He startled his doctors, parents, and everyone else in town—not only by walking in a few months' time, but also by using running as therapy for his burned legs. The healthcare community is wiser and better informed because of the triumphs of people like Cunningham.

Surgery and sophisticated therapies can accomplish a great deal, but ultimately, the patient needs the will to surmount the odds and push himself along the road to recovery. It's easy to feel depressed and discouraged, and it's easy to think about throwing in the towel.

Covered in sackcloth and ashes, the prognosticators of doom and gloom will always be with us. And their favorite sport will continue to be enlisting others to join their club.

When they approach you, just turn away. And remember people like Glen Cunningham, who rejected the experts, got out of bed, and walked and ran against all odds.

57

Celebrate the great moments

In the heart of New York's Times Square, there was once a
place called Birdland. It was the nation's premier center for
progressive jazz—a place where you could hear Chet Baker,
Stan Getz, J.J. Johnson, and other jazz legends, as well as the
big bands of Woody Herman, Stan Kenton, and Count Basie.
In those days, a guy named "Symphony Sid" had an all-night
jazz show that was a must for anyone who enjoyed music.

For me, the early 1950s was a time of major change. After
my graduation from college, Uncle Sam invited me and some
other young men for an all-expense-paid tour of Korea. In the
fall of 1952 I had just completed sixteen weeks of basic training and had two weeks' leave before being shipped out.

One night, wearing my Army uniform, I ventured into
Manhattan to hear some sounds at the famous Birdland.
Count Basie's band was playing that night, and singing at the
microphone was Ella Fitzgerald. For some reason, very few
people were at Birdland that night, and I had no trouble
getting a table.

As luck would have it, I found myself sitting one table away
from the great drummer, Buddy Rich. After a time, Rich
invited me to sit at his table, and later that evening, Count
Basie and Ella Fitzgerald joined the conversation.

When I got up to leave, Buddy Rich wouldn't let me pay a
cent. It was quite an evening for a young Army private out for
a final night on the town. Many years have passed since that

evening at Birdland. Buddy Rich went on to become one of the most gifted jazz drummers of this century, a self-taught genius who had never received any formal music training.

In 1987, I read in the newspaper that Buddy Rich had died of brain cancer. The obituaries also intimated that he was cantankerous, outspoken, and difficult. But that won't be the way I remember Buddy Rich. For one night, he made a poor, young Army private headed for Korea feel like a million dollars.

58

Learn to live passionately

The expression *a passion for living* suggests a person who enjoys every aspect of life to the fullest. Some people have the talent and good fortune to exude passion even when they're doing something as simple as drinking a cup of coffee, talking on the telephone, or taking a brisk walk.

Passion is connected to the drive to achieve success—as a spouse, a parent, an employee, or as a member of your community. Without this passion for success, very little can happen in your life. Having talked, worked, and traveled with many high achievers, I've learned that one characteristic they share in common is a passion for success and a passion for living.

Many experts insist that it's impossible to instill a passion for success in business. But I disagree. By leadership and example, strong executives can show workers the benefits of listening, hard work, drive, service, and keeping your word. In the same way, parents can instill the values of honesty, persistence, kindness, and cooperation in their children.

Not every executive, parent, teacher, or community leader is prepared to take on this mission. It means dedication, sacrifice, and the willingness to invest time in people. Above all, it means a passionate desire to help, serve, and support others.

59

Believe in something greater than yourself

"The world's held together day in and day out by mainly average people who believe in something bigger than themselves."

The words are those of author Don Snyder, writing in his book *Veteran's Park*. Don Snyder has written three books, yet he's virtually broke. His first book, *Veteran's Park*, was published in 1987, and was quickly followed by *From the Point* and *A Soldier's Disgrace*.

C. Michael Curtis, senior editor of *The Atlantic*, thought that *A Soldier's Disgrace* should have won a Pulitzer Prize. But the substance of Don's life hasn't been confined to writing.

In 1987, he and his wife founded the Maine Charitable Foundation to help families of terminally ill children who failed to qualify for federal assistance. In 1988, Snyder gave $100 to a Maine mother whose son had a brain tumor. A few years earlier, he had sent another boy to summer camp. On another occasion he gave a New Hampshire cancer patient $400 to fly to Tennessee for experimental treatments.

Although the Snyders have three children of their own, they willingly give needy families donations from their foundation's limited resources. The origin of their generosity is probably to be found in Snyder's upbringing.

Growing up in poverty, Snyder went to college on a need-based scholarship. After graduation, he tried a number of jobs but eventually returned to his first love: writing.

Although Snyder and his wife face ongoing financial problems, they are modest and unassuming about their kindness and generosity.

"I'm only trying to move an inch at a time," Snyder reflected. "Look at the families who adopt retarded children. Compared to them, I'm doing nothing. Or just think about the Bangor, Maine, surgeon who accepted an apple pie from a poor woman as payment for the thousands of dollars she owed him for hip operations. With me, it's just an inch."

Although Snyder was pleased to receive an invitation to teach at Colgate University, he worried about what the change in lifestyle would do to his family.

"For me, the best legacy you can give your children is this: 'He gave all his money away,' " said Snyder. "You've given them a light to follow—that's the way to happiness. Talk to old people and look and see who the happy ones are. They're the ones who gave it away."

The world is filled with people like Don Snyder and his wife. They're the generous givers of life, not its selfish takers. Love, mission, ethics, character, service, and a never-give-up attitude are integral to everything they do, and the world is a better place because of them.

60

Be grateful for what you've been given

My mother died when I was 5 years old, and until my dad remarried several years later, he was both my father and my mother. I felt lonely much of the time, because my father was a salesman, and he traveled throughout the Midwest.

But when he took me on one of his trips, it made up for all the time I had to spend by myself. To this day, I remember sitting in his lap singing songs and listening to stories about how lucky we were to live in this great country. It was a feeling and a message that would stay with me for more than fifty years. Today, when I hear about someone who feels the same way about this country, I remember my father, and I smile.

That happened during a 1987 episode of "60 Minutes," when I heard the great blind composer and singer Ray Charles say: "We are lucky in this country for the opportunities that we are given. We are blessed, because anyone who wants to put some time and effort into it can do well."

Suddenly, memories flooded over me, and I was sitting next to my dad, listening to him talk about America's boundless opportunities. The legacy of my father is probably the reason I have little use for people who engage in putdowns or who complain about life but offer few constructive solutions.

Few of such people venture onto the playing field of life, because they're usually afraid of risk, rejection, and defeat. Instead of choosing up sides, they elect to blame others for their problems and failures. Sometimes I feel sorry for these people. They've never felt the exhilaration that comes from carrying on an abiding love affair with this country.

No matter how profound our problems, this is a nation where dreams can be dreamed and turned into reality by hard work and plain grit. And even when people fail, they have the opportunity to stand up and start over again and again and again.

What more could we ask for?

61

Let's keep our priorities
in order

Mother Theresa is one of the greatest forces for good on this planet. She represents the highest standards of human compassion, and although she has few worldly possessions, she is wealthier than many billionaires. Her way of life is at once humbling and ennobling.

In the fall of 1989, Mother Theresa had a heart attack and was fitted with a pacemaker. Although she suffered another attack just a few days later, few newspapers reported it. Instead, there were stories on Zsa Zsa Gabor's altercation with a Beverly Hills policeman.

Somehow the song remains the same. Consider the trial and conviction of Leona Helmsley, who, along with her husband, Harry, is supposedly worth $5 billion. This woman reportedly took great joy in berating her employees and terminating them on the spot for even minor infractions. Blow-by-blow coverage of her trial in the national press detailed her apparently less-than-charitable way of dealing with people.

Then there's Mother Theresa, who invested most of her adult life caring for the deformed, the diseased, and the abandoned. She took in children who had been cast out by families and by society. She picked them up, cleaned them, caressed them, and gave them love.

Because of her belief in divine providence, she asks for and accepts no money. Having taken a vow of poverty, she has nothing of her own. But whenever she speaks, her plea for compassion and caring booms throughout the world.

Zsa Zsa Gabor and Leona Helmsley will likely fade in the public consciousness, but Mother Theresa will live forever. She represents everything great and good about healthcare, and her exemplary life should be celebrated.

62

Live a life of distinction

Some of the great dramas of human existence are reported in the obituary sections of local newspapers. In a few short paragraphs, you can sense the essence of a person's life.

Early in 1990, a local Chicago newspaper reported on the death of Gabriel Schwartz, M.D., who had died at the relatively young age of 52. Dr. Schwartz had developed the ALS Fund to research amyotrophic lateral sclerosis (Lou Gehrig's disease) and to assist people afflicted with the condition.

Dr. Schwartz's career got off to an outstanding start. A Phi Beta Kappa from Princeton University, he received his medical degree from Columbia University College of Physicians and Surgeons. A top internist, he was once the chief of medicine at a prominent Chicago hospital and professor of medicine at a leading medical school.

In the late 1980s, Dr. Schwartz's life changed forever. He was told that he had contracted ALS, the condition that would eventually claim his life. In the process of dying, Dr. Schwartz developed shimmering insights into the meaning of life, as reflected in the following memo to a close friend: "I have learned that life is fragile," he wrote. "We never know what is in store for us. We must make the most of every day, every moment. We cannot afford to procrastinate, or opportunity will pass us by. I have found a new meaning and pleasure in life by focusing on every interaction. I feel I can make a difference in the lives of others by just trying to communicate with them."

Dr. Schwartz had a kindred spirit in J.A. Wakefield, a World War II decorated hero who died at the age of 66. In 1981, he had retired from American Motors, where he was a janitor. But like Dr. Schwartz, Wakefield had fought one of life's greatest battles.

In 1944, during the battle of Montecassino in southern Italy, Wakefield single-handedly killed forty German soldiers with a machine gun and was awarded the Distinguished Service Cross and three Purple Hearts.

"He was instrumental in holding that hill for seventy-two hours," said his 84-year-old mother. "He had no one to feed the bullets into the machine gun."

Neither of these men lived a life of glamour or fame, and both died at a relatively young age. But in their own way, they had fought valiantly—one for freedom and the other for his own life. The world is a better place because of what they brought to it.

63

Go for your dreams

People who refuse to live up to society's expectations are a joy to be around. Whether you call them mavericks, eccentrics, or lovable nuts, they make this world a happier place. Because they revere and celebrate individuality, they embody a distinctly American spirit.

Such individuality is alive and well in Norfolk, Virginia, where a 51-year-old man named Mike recently put a successful mutual funds investment company and plans for a comfortable retirement on the back burner.

A husband and father at a young age, Mike was too busy raising a happy family to pursue his real dream: to get a college degree and to play college football. An outstanding player in high school, he was sought out by several big-name schools. But marriage, a baby, and a move to Virginia from Ohio put a damper on his plans.

Yet Mike never abandoned his dream to go to college and play football. Recently, he approached the coach of a local community college about trying out for the varsity team. He's already passed rigorous physicals and tests for endurance and strength, and it looks as if he has a fighting chance to make the team. He realizes he won't start, but it doesn't seem to matter to Mike. Being one step closer to his dream is all that counts.

Mike's acquaintances are probably convinced he's not playing with a full deck. But who cares what they think? Mike and other people like him realize that you're never too old to go for the brass ring and make every moment count.

Mike recognizes what others who are far younger may never understand: Every moment on earth is an opportunity to celebrate life and confront the myths and stereotypes that shatter our sense of self-esteem.

For too long, people over 50 have been calmed with such kindhearted words as, "Age gracefully" or "Be careful, you're too old for that." Instead, they should be counseled by the words of Welsh poet Dylan Thomas, who wrote: "Do not go gentle into that good night. Rage, rage against the dying of the light."

People in their 50s, 60s, 70s, or 80s should be allowed—and encouraged—to do whatever they want to do and to live life to the fullest.

To Mike and to other post-50 go-getters, there is only one piece of advice: Go for it. Your shining example will remind others that the 50-year mark is nothing more than a starting point for the next five decades of life.

64

Good manners make life easier and more pleasurable

Good manners are at the very core of a civilized society, because good manners demand that you treat others with dignity and respect. Unfortunately, the "survival of the fittest" ethic that seems to pervade popular culture dictates that the ruder and pushier you become, the more you will succeed. But most of us know that isn't true.

Whether you're trying to persuade customers to purchase your products and services or to convince your spouse to go to your favorite vacation spot, good manners make good sense. In this competitive arena, having the right product and price may no longer be enough, according to Ann Marie Sabath, who writes etiquette columns for the *Cincinnati Enquirer* and the *Washington Times*.

"Whether you are meeting a client for the first time, conducting business over lunch, or making telephone calls in transit, one thing is certain: Your actions are being watched," she writes.

Her advice applies equally well to social relationships and to exchanges in the realms of education, entertainment, and politics. The reality is that good manners and respect for the other person are a kind of evidence. No matter what your objective or main point, good manners support your case.

Unfortunately, good manners don't always come naturally

or as a complement to a college diploma or M.B.A. degree. Good manners need to be taught and continually reinforced through training and coaching.

Some of the most courteous people I've known never made it beyond high school. But somewhere along the line, they picked up the basics of treating people well, and, as a result, they enjoyed incredible success.

In today's world, getting along with people is essential, and good manners help smooth the way.

65

Respect people and listen to them

My father was the best salesman I've ever known. He loved people and doted on his customers—and his best customers often became his best friends.

When I was 5, my mother died, and my father started to take me on some of his business trips in his Packard. My father was disciplined, organized, well-liked and a gentleman—and I loved every minute of being with him. Even when I entered my teens, I would often make sales calls with him on weekends. He loved life, he loved his job, he loved his family, and he loved his country.

Spending so much time with my father, I naturally observed how he treated people—from customers and friends, to casual acquaintances and strangers. I learned a lot from him, but his greatest lesson was this: Treat the "little people"—those without power or prestige—as well as or even better than those people with important positions and social standing.

When I traveled with my father, or even if we were playing a round of golf, I was always impressed with his courteous treatment of bellhops, waiters, janitors, warehouse people, and other members of the working class. He went out of his way to be natural and courteous—not because he wanted a perk or extra bit of service, but because it was his nature and his style.

He used the same approach with his colleagues at work.

He shared their triumphs and their failures, and even though he ended up with the top job in his company, he never lost his ability to make people feel appreciated and valued. The image of my father—and the thousands of encounters he had with the world's "little people"—is etched in my memory forever.

There are some exceptions, but when people are respected and listened to, they respond with affection and appreciation. In the hustle and bustle of business, this basic tenet of life is sadly and too often forgotten.

Remember this as you climb the ladder of success: The higher you climb, the harder you may fall. Said another way: "Be kind and gracious to people on the way up, because you just may meet them again on the way down." And if that happens, the way they respond to you will probably mirror the way you initially treated them.

66

Teach your children well

Over the years, leaders from business, government, education, and the arts have read dry, lifeless speeches to college graduation classes. In 1988, when my son graduated with an M.B.A. from Northwestern University's Kellogg Graduate School of Management, I wanted to tell him the essential ingredients of success that he would never hear at his graduation ceremony.

+ M.B.A. degrees are no guarantee of success. Your degree may give you the illusion that you know more than you do. As you begin or resume your career, be humble enough to listen and learn. If you allow people to help you, they'll go out of their way to do so. But if you give people the impression that you know everything, you'll probably be left alone.

+ Keep your word, and tell the truth. Although you may sometimes want to gloss over the truth, resist the temptation. Never compromise your standards or your self-respect. As you progress through your career, you'll quickly learn that your self-respect is probably your most important asset. Remember that you have to live with yourself twenty-four hours a day, every day, and if you don't like yourself, the days will be long and empty.

+ As you climb the management ladder, learn to be gentle with people and to understand their wishes, hopes, and dreams. Other people are just like you—they need help and encouragement.

✦ Never be conned into thinking that caring and concern for others is a sign of weakness. People who are unafraid to demonstrate their compassion and concern for others are usually revered for their character, wisdom, and good will. And they tend to lead happy and fulfilled lives.

✦ Keep money and material possessions in perspective. Compensation, benefits, and perks are important. But never let money become your master. The world has its share of ignorant, insensitive, and explosive people who have more money than they can spend. Money never bought their happiness, satisfaction, or peace of mind.

✦ Remember that in the end, only three things in life matter: Love of family, love of friends, and love of work.

✦ Keep your life simple, and don't get caught up in flash, hoopla, and glitz.

✦ Be passionate about life, and consider yourself blessed to be a citizen of this country.

67

Know what success really is

Last week, a young lady I know and love told me she felt inadequate because she wasn't successful. When I asked her what she meant by success, she hemmed and hawed, but really couldn't describe it.

Frankly, I think a lot of people are like her: frustrated because they haven't attained success, but without a clear idea of what it really is. Let me explain.

Success isn't flying around the country on a jet. It's not staying in a sumptuous hotel room, watching TV alone. Success isn't becoming an executive so you can lord it over people who don't have your drive or ambition or talent. Success isn't living in a big house or wearing a fur coat or an $800 suit or driving an expensive car. These are simply material things, and on a scale of one to ten, they don't rate very high if you're really successful.

Let me tell you what I think success really is. It's giving love and hugs and kisses to the most important people in your life— your family. It's feeling good about yourself and working hard to be a better person. It's being a good parent or son or daughter, as well as being a good citizen.

I admire truly successful people who care about other people and are gentle with those who have less clout and power than they do. I admire people who play life straight and don't cheat on their families or friends or colleagues.

Success is standing for something that has meaning—like

honesty and integrity. Success is all of these things and more, but it's not the glitz and glamour that people think of as the trappings of success. We seem to have gotten our priorities mixed up as to what success is, but it's definitely not the size of your paycheck.

Whom do I consider successful people? Heading my list are nurses, who day in and day out do things that absolutely mesmerize my sensitivities. Caring for a dying child or working in an oncology unit or an operating room are just a few of the things these outstandingly successful people do. And most of them still make less than a garbage collector.

Then there are the social workers and psychologists and volunteers who every day advise people who need help, and they aren't paid very well either. Paramedics are also high on my list. Every day they save countless lives with their heroic acts of caring.

And there are teachers and policemen and servicemen and scores of others who don't make a lot of money, but without them our society couldn't function. Of course, there are also successful business people who give of their time and energies without pay on school boards and other organizations, to help make this society better for all of us. Therefore, the true meaning of success, in my mind, is being a decent human being who cares about others.

Finally, success can also be measured by how much someone cares about this great country of ours. It doesn't cost anything to give a darn about the good old U.S.A., but in our so-called sophisticated, chic circles it's not always considered the thing to do.

That's too bad, because those people who feel that way miss the whole point of what being a success is all about. It's caring about others, and that kind of thinking permeates the very fabric of this nation and makes me proud to be an American.

May you all be successful.

68
Appreciate the privilege of working

Some people have a passion for working. Others do not. Think about how many people get up in the morning dreading to go to work. As a matter of fact, too many people today feel that the world owes them a living without their working for it. The work ethic which built this country has become a rare trait, so when people display that trait, they should be encouraged and nurtured.

On a recent New York business trip I had a very interesting cab ride. The cab driver was a recent arrival in this country from communist Poland. I'll never forget his comments, because they made me realize how much too many Americans take for granted.

As best I can, I'll paraphrase what this wonderful gentleman said to me in his broken English: "You people are very lucky here, because so many of you have the privilege of working. Too many of us in Poland are not given that opportunity, and we simply have given up hope."

The key words are "the privilege of working." I'll never forget them, because they are so true. I believe that it's a privilege to have employment. It is a privilege to be an American and be part of this great country. And I consider it a distinct privilege to work with so many talented colleagues, day in and day out, producing each issue of *Modern Healthcare*.

Remember that work is not a right, nor is it an unwelcome duty. It is, indeed, a privilege.

Meeting Marketing Challenges

We're taking customers seriously . . . instead of telling people what's best for them, we're now asking them what they want.

69

Creating a marketing culture in the organization

In many healthcare organizations, marketing was never integrated into the organization's strategic plan, and many marketers were never pushed to operate with a bottom-line focus.

For one thing, we spent too much money on advertising—and we did it with no research, evaluation, or cost/benefit analysis. Does this mean we should abandon all advertising? Of course not. But it sure doesn't mean that we advertise a program for two months—and then stop dead in our tracks because no new patients walk though the hospital's front door. After all, we're not operating a fast-food restaurant. Clip-out coupons don't always bring in patients.

What we need to realize is that when we get into the advertising game—and the marketing game—we're in for the duration. It's a long-term strategy and a long-term investment—and it only works when you hold people accountable.

Does that mean holding an ax over the head of the vice president of marketing and telling him or her to produce or else? Of course not. If marketing's going to do its job, marketers need to build a marketing culture, and senior executives need to support it.

What do I mean? Simply that marketers can't do everything. We have to create a culture where everybody in the organization becomes a marketer and a salesperson for that organization—and that includes people in finance—from the bookkeeper and accounts payable clerk to the systems analyst.

Everyone needs to accept accountability for what happens in, through, and with the organization. And what does that require? In my mind, it means better planning, better controls, and better strategies for evaluation.

I spend a lot of time talking to vendor and provider CEOs, and it shocks me to find out how many have never written a business plan and how many don't even seem to have a marketing plan.

Oh sure, they have something called a strategic plan—but most of the time these things seem to sit on shelves and gather dust. But how many organizations or for-profit ventures have business plans that are supported by one- and five-year financial plans, and marketing and human resources plans? The sad reality is, not too many.

It doesn't do any good to talk about controls and accountability unless you have solid marketing objectives and market information. But how many organizations have marketing objectives that are measurable, realistic, specific, and acceptable to everybody involved? Once again, not too many.

70

Senior management and marketing

et's take a little quiz: (1) Does your CEO see marketing as an expense—or as an investment? (2) Does your CEO equate advertising with marketing? (3) Does your CEO assume that if you run an advertisement in a Sunday supplement, patients will come through your doors on Monday? In other words does he—or she—have unrealistic expectations of marketing? (4) Does your CEO see marketing as a short-term fix rather than a long-term strategy? (5) Does your CEO view marketing as a separate department or area of the hospital and not as a way of doing business that's integrated within the organiation? (6) Is your CEO interested in preserving the status quo rather than risking a failure?

If you were nodding your head while I asked these questions, guess what? You're not alone. Marketers continually complain about the lack of commitment of senior management to marketing, and that CEOs and COOs just don't understand it.

As I travel around the country, I'm amazed at how many sensitive, intelligent, and otherwise capable senior executives don't understand marketing—and don't seem to want to understand. Many have never even done a business plan—let alone a marketing plan. And let's face it: Traditional M.H.A. programs have really missed the boat when it comes to teaching marketing as an approach to doing business.

And this is, after all, a risk-averse industry. Every industry has created its version of the Edsel. But did Ford say that it would never advertise again when the Edsel bombed? Did it fire its entire marketing staff or shut down the marketing department?

As Art Sturm, president of Sturm Communications, a Chicago ad agency, says, "Failure doesn't mean you throw out the discipline." In other words, just because you have high mortality in a certain surgery doesn't mean you stop doing it. Instead, you try to make things better.

71

Go out and get your fair share of the market

D id you ever hear the story about the man who lived by the side of the road and sold hot dogs? He sold very good hot dogs, and had signs on the highway telling people how good his hot dogs tasted.

He stood by the side of the road and called out, "Buy a hot dog, Mister?" People bought so many of his hot dogs that the man increased his meat and bun orders and even bought a bigger stove, so he could satisfy his customers' demands. In fact, he got so busy he brought his son home from college to help in the family business.

That's when things changed. His son said, "Father, don't you watch TV or read the papers? The economy is slowing down, the European situation is unsettled, and there's talk of a recession coming."

The father thought that his college-educated son should know what he was talking about, so he decided to prepare for bad business. He cut down his meat and bun orders, took down his highway signs, and no longer bothered to stand by the roadside and ask people to buy his hot dogs.

Guess what? Sales fell almost immediately. "You're right, son," said the father. "It looks like we're in the middle of a serious recession."

This little vignette was from one of a series of four ads that ran in *Advertising Age*, a sister publication to *Modern Healthcare*, back in 1980. I've never forgotten them. The story of the hot dog man is my favorite, because in a very entertaining way it delivered the message that if you stop selling your customers today, in all probability they'll stop buying from you tomorrow. It's simple, it's basic, it's true.

Yet as I travel around the country, I run into some thinking that doesn't make sense at all. Interest rates are stable, unemployment is low, the healthcare industry is growing and diversifying at an astonishing pace, but I'm hearing things like, "You know, this industry has been in a boom period for the last ten years. We don't think it's going to last another ten years, so we're waiting and watching and taking a conservative approach to business."

Now, I have to tell you something. The person who told me this is with a company founded by one of the most aggressive entrepreneurs I've ever known. A salesman's salesman, he always seemed to be in the field, going from account to account helping his people make sales.

And he promoted his company through advertising. Not an ad here and there, now and then, but sometimes in one issue he'd run six to eight ads on his company's products. When I'd be talking to CEOs or administrators, they'd mention the ads they saw in *Modern Healthcare* and tell me what a great guy this person was. They would comment on how well his company must be doing because they were able to run so many ads. Invariably they'd say he had visited them a week or two ago or was coming in another few weeks.

If he knew the conservative approach his company is taking now, he wouldn't stand for it. Successful salespeople for successful companies don't listen to doom-and-gloomers or take a wait-and-see attitude. They simply go out and sell their products and services.

Friends, don't stand still, and don't procrastinate. Go out and get your fair share of the market. It's there, but you have to go out and sell it. Remember that you have to let people know that you're still in business. Make plenty of sales calls and advertise. Winners are positive thinkers.

72

Take a creative view of trade show exhibitions

If you're an executive, you can use trade show exhibitions to make valuable contacts and get acquainted with new products and services.

The days when throngs of people filled the aisles at industry trade shows are long gone. Successful exhibitors need to rethink their basic approach to these meetings and the kinds of exhibits they choose to develop. The industry is in a period of unprecedented change, but some vendors and consultants seem unwilling to acknowledge or accept it.

Making an appearance by having a booth or displaying your company colors isn't good enough anymore. Trade show exhibits are a critical component of any marketing strategy. What's needed? Vendors and consultants who depend on these exhibits to generate business need to recognize the reality of decreasing attendance and opt for quality of contact instead of quantity. That may mean a reevaluation of overall show strategy and the type of booths used.

At the same time, the professionals who run these conventions must develop outstanding educational programs so that executives feel compelled to attend even when budgets are tight. What's more, these show managers need to recognize that vendors are customers who generate significant advertising dollars by exhibiting at their convention. All too often, vendors are ignored or treated shabbily instead of being welcomed as paying customers.

What's the bottom line? Vendors and show managers need to work together so their mutual goals are recognized and achieved. Although there's clear evidence that business has changed, many people still insist on the tried-and-true methods of the past. In spite of good intentions, they will no longer work.

Exhibitors and show managers who stay in tune and in touch will see their business prosper, but those who refuse to wake up may see their shows decline and possibly fade away.

73

Market research is listening

Market research hasn't fulfilled its potential. As Pat Mages points out, we don't do it consistently—and we don't do it with all of our customers: patients, families, visitors, physicians, payers, and employees.

Pat has one quote that I really like: "Marketing research is listening in the finest sense."

We may listen to expectant parents and former maternity patients when we expand our maternity area, but have we applied the same thinking to dealing with our payers? The answer is: not nearly enough.

And there's another thing: People continue to buy market research on the basis of price—almost as if it's a commodity. These days it seems as if we're doing more market research, but enjoying it less. More dollars are spent on market research today than ten or twelve years ago, but the research doesn't always drive decision making in the way it should.

Maybe it's because we use research as a tactic, not as a strategy. But what do we really need? Research that will help us understand our role in the marketplace. Why? Because when all is said and done, marketing is a servant of the organization's long-term interests. Looked at in terms of the language of battle, it's a long-term ground war strategy.

74

Concentrate your advertising

If you're an executive, scrutinize advertisements to learn about new products and services. After investing hundreds of thousands of dollars in advertising campaigns, many healthcare executives have lost respect for the medium. Rather than making prudent adjustments in their ad budgets, they've abandoned advertising entirely.

But the medium is rarely the culprit. In most cases, advertising was simply misused. Vendors have spent years learning the lessons of effective advertising.

Here's one standard piece of advice: Invest in concentration. That's the opinion of the American Business Press, a New York-based organization created to help advertisers use business publications more effectively.

Out of five publications within a field, the leading publication delivers more than half of the coverage—an average of 66 percent—provided by all five publications together. And because cost and coverage aren't added at the same rate, succeeding publications add increasingly fewer readers. The fifth publication adds only 3 percent new unduplicated readers, and each of these new readers costs eighteen times as much to reach as a reader of the leading publication.

The bottom line is this: Concentration of your advertising dollars forces prospects, clients, and customers to focus their attention in what has become an increasingly competitive and cluttered marketplace.

75

Advertising is an investment, not an expense

Advertising is the cornerstone of any successful, well-rounded marketing program. Advertising produces sales, and without advertising, a company can quickly lose its hard-earned market share.

Unfortunately, many top executives fail to believe in or understand advertising simply because marketing and advertising executives haven't invested time in promoting its benefits to management.

A key marketing executive once called me in a panic to report that he had recently begun to report to his company's chief "numbers cruncher"—a man who had put all advertising on hold because he viewed it as an "expensive luxury."

Another ad agency executive told me that a reorganization within a client organization resulted in an attorney being put in charge of all marketing and advertising. Both of these individuals could see the signs of doom. They knew the accountant and the attorney would decide to save a few bucks to produce a better bottom line, with little concern for millions of dollars in lost sales.

But who's to blame? Perhaps we should take a look in the mirror. The reason accountants, engineers, and attorneys don't understand advertising is that sales, marketing and public relations professionals have failed to take the time to explain, educate, and convince them of advertising's value. Unfortunately, we're so busy with management routine and marketing our own products and services that we forget how little our colleagues know about marketing and advertising.

The bottom line is this: The incredible power of advertising must be promoted over and over again. As sales and marketing professionals, we must make a constant, concerted effort to sell non-believers on advertising's promise. Let them know that advertising is not an expense, but an investment that will help keep your organization profitable and alive.

76

Invest in advertising

To advertise or not to advertise? Does advertising really move healthcare products and services? These are the questions that go through the minds of healthcare executives as they contemplate the appropriate role for advertising and promotion in the future of their organizations.

Unfortunately, too many healthcare executives view advertising as a tawdry and wasteful expenditure of money, or as an unwelcome intrusion on valuable management time. But why?

Those of us who sell advertising space and time, and who consider ourselves advertising and sales professionals, can take at least some of the blame for the confusion and cynicism that surrounds advertising.

Advertising sales representatives, account executives and supervisors in advertising and public relations agencies, and publishers must share the responsibility for failing to communicate advertising's merits—not only to our clients and prospects, but also to the people who work for us.

Too many people in advertising have little or no training and, even worse, have not yet paid their dues. The majority have no experience in watching something as basic as a point-of-sale promotion move a product. They might be able to design a sassy ad campaign, but they've never viewed the campaign's payoff by spending time in the field with clients and users.

Advertising is a must for any organization that wants to succeed, including healthcare organizations. Advertising should be treated with respect—not as an uninvited relative who decides to stay for a week, but as a celebrated guest.

Here are only some of advertising's benefits:

✦ Advertising tells an organization's story—with accuracy, color, and drama.

✦ Advertising delivers measurable results—when management takes the time to engage in measurement and evaluation.

✦ Advertising supports a sales force by reaching top potential clients and customers.

✦ Advertising makes customers aware of your products and services.

✦ Advertising creates or brings to the surface a need, so that customers will buy the services you choose to promote.

✦ Advertising reminds your customers that you're ready to do business and serve their needs.

If that doesn't convince you, just consider the consequences of not advertising. Competition is keen, and everyone claims to have the best products and services. If you fail to keep your name in the forefront and maintain your presence in the marketplace, your customers might be tempted to look for another organization.

There's no profound secret to good advertising. It should tell your organization's story in language that's simple, clear, direct, concrete, and specific, and be directed to critical customers, clients, and prospects.

Most important, advertising should be viewed as a key component of your marketing plan, not as a tactic or trick you discard in an economic downturn. Businesses that advertise during periods of recession capture a stronger share of the market when the economy takes an upward swing. The same lesson is true for healthcare.

77

Invest in repeat advertising, not in single ads

The message is clear, and it's been validated throughout the healthcare industry: Repeat advertising, and not a scattered series of single ads, is the key to successful advertising campaigns.

According to McGraw-Hill's Laboratory of Advertising Research, advertisers who inserted ads every month averaged 184 advertising impressions among readers, while ads that appeared every other month produced an average of 94 impressions. Not surprising, those that appeared every third month registered only 64 impressions.

And what does this mean? Simply that you can't move people to buy with a single advertisement; instead, you must sell to a passing parade of buying influences. This situation is especially true in the healthcare industry, where as much as 30 percent of a hospital's staff may turn over in a single year.

The bottom line is this: People you've already sold to move on to other work environments, and new people move into their jobs. That's as good a reason as any to repeat effective advertisements.

78

Never promise more than you can deliver

You may capture the reader's interest, but if you're unable to deliver on your promises, you're dead. Several years ago an advertisement for a major airline portrayed an executive lounging in a large, luxurious seat, his shoeless feet resting on a pillow, a drink in his hand, and a smile on his face.

Those of us who travel regularly are still waiting to receive that level of service from a domestic carrier. Simply stated, that advertisement failed to represent the world of the contemporary business traveler. All too often, we're afflicted with delays, lost baggage, bad food, rude employees, and turbulence.

Although the intent of the ad was to encourage the business traveler to choose one airline, it probably had the opposite effect. Few battle-scarred veterans of business travel would be likely to buy the too-good-to-be-true message of that advertisement. Like I did, they probably saw it as unrealistic and condescending.

Executives who read trade publications, or consumers who read community publications, are no exception. When they see ads that ignore the nitty-gritty, shirt-sleeves environment they struggle in every day or that promise more than they can deliver, they're put off and even a little offended. Pie in the sky or idealized portrayals just don't work.

Executives and consumers have one thing in common. Both are seeking products and services that will help them survive. Smart, realistic, and experienced, they want facts, not fluff. And they want information and data, not empty slogans. There are plenty of sales to be made in the healthcare industry, but advertising messages must be simple, on target, and appeal to readers' interests.

79

Follow fundamental principles of sound advertising

What makes an ad effective? All too often people get so caught up in the glitz and production values that they lose sight of the basic message and the reader. To that end, you would do well to follow these principles:

✦ Keep ads simple and straightforward. Most people won't take the time to read a lot of unnecessary verbiage.

✦ Rely on testimonials. In a close-knit industry like healthcare, a few kind words from a colleague can go a long way in developing an effective case for a product or service.

✦ Don't be afraid to discuss price or cost savings. Everybody wants to save money, and that's especially true for healthcare executives under the gun of prospective pricing.

✦ Make a point of service and follow-through. Just about every consumer wants to patronize vendors who are willing and able to back up their products, and healthcare executives are no exception. In this tight economic climate, executives want suppliers who can stretch an investment through good service.

80

Salespeople make it happen

Over the years I've concluded that top salespeople are really a different breed. They don't fit any stereotypes, and in some ways they might be considered a little strange. That's because they march to a different drummer than most other people.

It puzzles me why anyone would want to go into sales in the first place, because in today's competitive environment it's filled with heavy doses of rejection. And in a lot of companies, salespeople aren't really treated the way they should be, even though they are the very lifeblood of any organization. Without salespeople selling product, nothing happens.

Money is usually considered the prime motivator of salespeople. Now, I don't disagree that money is important to anyone. It's one way of measuring one's performance and skills and, on a pragmatic basis, it pays the bills, sends the kids to college, and lets one lead a pleasant life.

But I'm going to tell you one of the best-kept secrets in the world. Most top salespeople are in sales not for the money, but because they are fierce competitors and love the field of battle. Their greatest moments come when they make the sale and beat out a competitor. That wish to excel and win is too often overlooked and misunderstood by companies and sales consultants.

Sure, money is important, but so is a positive environment, leadership (notice I don't use the word management), and a

167

willingness to get out of the way and let people sell.

Now, that's an important point. Most sales training tells people what they can't do. It tells them how much money they can't spend and all the rules and regulations they must abide by. It tells people to be team members and to conform.

Some of these criteria are absolutely necessary, but I have to tell you that too much sales training is too regimented, too lackluster, too conformist. Even though salespeople will put up with it, deep down in their hearts they resent it.

So what am I saying? Sure, teach the basics of your products and services, and make sure they understand their compensation package. But if you really want to appeal to the best in salespeople, talk about honor and ethics and the joy of competition. Give them the best inspirational leadership, and make sure they are treated fairly every step of the way.

They are a tough lot. By nature they are idealists, they are dreamers, they are spontaneous, and they want to believe in their company. And I find them very patriotic individuals who truly believe in the American way of life. If given half a chance, they will make sales you didn't even think possible. But they need encouragement to be creative, and they shouldn't feel afraid to fail, because that's all part of the learning process.

The bottom line is this. Instead of a kick in the pants, most quality salespeople respond better to a pat on the shoulder. Furthermore, if you want to set a sales force really humming, be a boss who treats them with dignity and respect. Quality leaders understand that truly exceptional salespeople have exceptionally high standards that need constant nurturing. It's the formula for success.

Salespeople make it happen.

81

Focus on the essence of sales success

What makes a good salesperson? The key ingredient for anyone planning a career in sales and marketing is self-esteem. Sales-training seminars, "dress for success" workshops, and five-star product lines can't create a good salesperson unless that person begins with a strong sense of self.

Unfortunately, too few people understand who they are and what they can contribute to their professions, their industry, and to society. Here are the other success ingredients:

✦ Learn the art of listening. It's the most critical skill for anyone who wants to become a top-flight salesperson. Unfortunately, many salespeople enter a client's office and begin talking before their rear end hits the chair. Top salespeople always listen to their customers' needs. Marginal salespeople, in contrast, talk and talk and talk—usually about themselves.

✦ Maintain eye contact. Winning salespeople make their prospects feel as if they're the most important people in the world. If your eyes wander, or if you look away, clients and customers will assume you've lost interest.

✦ Don't knock the competition. Discredit others, and you'll be helping their product or service, not yours. Slamming competitors might work in the short term, but in the long haul it's self-defeating.

✦ Ask for the order. Some of the most successful salespeople could be even more successful if they asked for the order. Several years ago, a McGraw-Hill study revealed that more than half of all salespeople who made more than $50,000 annually failed to ask for the order. Why? Apparently, they were too embarrassed to ask people for "money."

✦ Extend appreciation. If you get an order, never forget to say thank-you. Then, make every effort to follow up with the best possible service.

✦ Let your product shine. Make your product or service—not you—the center of attention. Unfortunately, some salespeople believe that it's more important to sell themselves than their product or service. But that's not what good selling is all about. Concentrate on your product and service, and give it star status.

✦ Keep your word. Top earners in the sales profession keep their word. When they promise something, they do it. They have a high regard for themselves, for their reputations, for their companies, and for their products and services.

✦ Be honest. Top salespeople don't try to skim a few bucks off their expense account just because they can get away with it. People who sell need high standards of integrity and honor, and that comes from a strong sense of self-esteem—feeling good about yourself and what you do.

✦ Exercise discipline both personally and professionally. Strong salespeople are up early in the morning, and they make their first sales call as early as possible.

✦ Don't make excuses—especially to your boss. Strong salespeople admit their mistakes and get on with their jobs. They're too busy planning their next sales call to waste time making excuses. Marginal salespeople, in contrast, tend to blame their failures on everybody but themselves.

✦ Keep your boss informed. Top salespeople make sure their bosses are never surprised or embarrassed by their actions. In fact, they're more likely to view their boss as a colleague, ally, or mentor. Marginal salespeople, in contrast, abhor accountability and invest a great deal of time and energy in cutting corners, sneaking around, and short-circuiting management.

✦ Maintain enthusiasm and a positive attitude. All top salespeople accept every new situation as a challenge. No matter what the odds, they persist, and they don't surrender without a fight. If a prospect rejects their request, they look at it, not as a defeat, but as an opportunity to exercise their skills of persuasion.

✦ Get out and make calls. Top salespeople pound the pavement and keep the phone lines burning. They understand that the most critical aspect of their job is eyeball-to-eyeball contact with a customer, and to that end they'll go anywhere, anytime, to make a call. What's more, they're enthusiastic about the opportunity.

82

Show customers you're concerned

The healthcare field never realized the magnitude of Karl Bays' contribution until he left Baxter in 1987 to become CEO of IC Industries.

Karl Bays was a "salesman." Blessed with charisma and boundless energy, he had come up through the sales ranks. In doing so, he had handled his share of rejections and understood from personal experience what it took to make a sale.

No ivory-tower, corner-office executive, Karl never forgot what it meant to look customers straight in the eye and greet them with a firm handshake. No matter how busy his calendar, he always managed to return to the field to make calls and sales.

But fellow sales professionals weren't the only people to appreciate the magic of Karl Bays. Over the years, I've heard CEOs of healthcare organizations give relatively low marks to the performance of healthcare vendors.

These executives generally expressed disappointment that vendors misunderstood even the most basic problems faced by providers.

More often than not, one of the CEOs in these discussions would bring up the name of Karl Bays, and everyone's head would begin to nod in assent. What they acknowledged and appreciated about Karl Bays was his ability to represent his company with distinction and, at the same time, reassure customers that he was concerned about their problems. He let his customers know that he cared about their life's work and that he would help them overcome their challenges with strong products and solid negotiating. If Karl Bays had a secret to success, that was it.

83

Offer creative cost-saving opportunities

If you're an executive, don't be afraid to request creative solutions to your problems. If you're a sales representative or a consultant, be prepared to go the distance. Instead of just responding to your clients' requests, volunteer your own creative solutions.

Back in 1984, pharmaceuticals were cited by healthcare executives as the product category that offered the greatest potential for cost savings. In another few years, executives might flag another product or service for cost containment, retrenchment, or development.

The point is this: The opportunities for creative problem solving in healthcare are out there. Vendors and consultants need to be aware and savvy enough to discover and act on them.

Consider this example. Back in 1984, a vendor determined that property stolen from hospitals averaged $750 annually per hospital bed. But he didn't stop there. Instead, he carefully calculated how his equipment could nip 80 to 90 percent off these acts of theft and how, in the first year alone, the savings would more than pay for the purchase of his equipment.

Now that's smart selling.

84

Don't be a loser

Aren't you getting tired of reading articles and books telling you how to make a million dollars a month? But if everyone achieves success, many of us will have to work harder.

That's why people need to understand how to fail and lose through the following five-point plan:

✦ FAILURE SECRET NUMBER ONE: Don't listen to other people. Talk over your clients' heads and interrupt them as many times as possible if they try to ask a question. Above all, try to keep your customers and prospects ignorant. On the other hand, never let your own ignorance and stupidity stand in your way. If you're not interested in discussing your products or services, then feel free to talk about politics, religion, race, or sex.

✦ FAILURE SECRET NUMBER TWO: Keep your boss in the dark. You probably know everything you need to know about sales, so resist any direction and advice. And don't forget to remind your colleagues about how much you know and what you've achieved.

✦ FAILURE SECRET NUMBER THREE: Look the part. Make yourself the star of a client visit by wearing flashy clothes and lots of gold jewelry. And don't forget to have a few drinks at lunch so you're totally relaxed when you see your client.

✦ FAILURE SECRET NUMBER FOUR: Stay off the

team. Never admit to being a team member—it smacks of weakness. And if you make a mistake, be sure to blame a colleague, the federal government, the weather, or the decline of American culture for what happened. It's an excellent way to win the attention and respect of management and your colleagues.

✦ FAILURE SECRET NUMBER FIVE: Invest a lot of time in feeling sorry for yourself. Try not to look on the bright side of things. Instead, concentrate your full attention on what's wrong, or even better, on what could go wrong. If someone demonstrates zest and excitement about his work, dismiss him immediately as a naive romantic. In that way, you can help him feel just as badly as you do.

85

Make the sales call the center of your professional life

One of the toughest jobs of sales managers is motivating people to make sales calls. Unfortunately, too many sales people enjoy the compensation and perks afforded by the sales profession without really taking pleasure in the sales lifestyle.

The sales call must become the center of a salesperson's life. Making a sales call is not unlike going out on a baseball diamond or tennis court. Whatever it takes, you need to be prepared and motivated to execute the call. Some salespeople have even been known to say a brief prayer before entering a room.

Top sales performers enjoy looking good and feeling good, and they have an uncanny ability to make their customers and clients feel good, too. Although top performers don't necessarily wear expensive clothes or tell clever stories, they tend to be neat in their appearance and polite in their approach. Above all, they understand that listening helps customers and clients feel positively about themselves and about the interaction.

Top sales people also have an almost contagious enthusiasm. They project a zest for their products and their clients' needs. But even more important, they have a zest for life and quickly dismiss downtrodden colleagues who complain about the tough hand that life has dealt. Top salespeople absorb the energy and enthusiasm of people around them. Usually, they've learned from experience that the best antidote for rejection and a disappointing bottom line is a well-executed sales call.

86

Ask for the order

Being a good salesperson requires discipline, mental dexterity, and the ability to spring back from rejection. Unfortunately, many companies continue to operate with stereotypes about five-star sales professionals and concentrate more on superficial features than on qualities of personality and character.

Being gregarious, well-dressed, physically attractive, and clever with words doesn't guarantee sales success. Although these people have all the right ingredients, they might not bring in results. Other salespeople are modest, plain, and shy, but they deliver sales results. Why?

The outgoing, attractive go-getter may have forgotten the four most important words in sales: "I want your order." Asking for the order is so basic to the sales transaction that it's a wonder that any sales professional would forget it.

Test the theory for yourself. Ask your customers how many salespeople who call on them ask for the order. "I've had sales people call me, give me a soup-to-nuts presentation, thank me for my time, and then leave without asking for the order," said one buyer of millions of dollars in advertising. "They must think I'm supposed to get the idea of giving them business through osmosis."

As cited earlier in this book, a study completed by McGraw-Hill in the mid-1980s confirmed this observation. Even salespeople who made more than $50,000 annually often failed to ask for the order for one reason: They were too embarrassed to ask people for money.

Perhaps you work with a group of terrific salespeople who are highly motivated and will travel anywhere you ask them. Unfortunately, if they're not coached to ask for the order on every sales call, all the positive personal attributes in the world won't make a difference.

87

Give the people you work with the attention they deserve

Much of what I've learned about sales over the last thirty-plus years has been by trial and error. Like football players or dancers, salespeople can benefit from practice.

But the real test comes when they go out onto the playing field or the stage, or into the offices of customers. That's when you see their drive, energy, and dedication.

Just as critical to sales success is having a strong boss. Good people beget good people. If salespeople can learn from quality role models, they'll maximize their opportunities for success. But all too often sales managers compensate for personal anxieties and insecurities by trying to take advantage of their people. They think they can motivate through fear and threats of reprisals. But they're wrong.

Even if intimidation works in the short term, its long-term result is cynicism and despair. People who find themselves in a negative environment tend to update their resumes and renew their industry acquaintances.

Salespeople don't need bullying. They need positive reinforcement, attention, and training. Strong sales managers breed loyalty, commitment, and quality in their sales organizations. That, in turn, produces high performance and sales records year after year. What's more, these sales organizations have little turnover, because managers invest time in working the field with their people.

Sales managers need to make their people feel important for one reason: Their people are important. If you're a sales manager—or if you aspire to be one—help your people understand that the company's success is dependent on their performance.

88

Adapt your schedule to the customers' needs

One day, when I was buying elbow pads in a local sports store, the owner commented on the difficulties he had with suppliers who wanted him to sign two- to three-year agreements.

And even when he signed these agreements, he claimed that he rarely reaped the benefits in extras or value-added service. According to this independent entrepreneur, service from suppliers was abysmal.

"A salesman came to see me when I was busy with customers, so I told him to come back after 5:00 P.M.," he said. "But he never came back. A few days later I called the guy's boss, who told me that he wouldn't let his salesmen work after five o'clock or on weekends because he wanted them to lead normal lives, and that unless I could see people during normal business hours, I couldn't carry his line. Today that company is bankrupt."

The sporting goods store owner went on to complain that many sales jobs, paying $30,000 to $40,000 annually plus a car and expense account, go begging because "nobody wants to work."

He reported that one company had initiated a program in which each salesperson had to make a minimum of six calls per day. Because salespeople had to limit their calls to fifteen or thirty minutes, they left behind a lot of brochures but made very few long-term relationships. Although this company had once been known as "the Cadillac of the industry," it was now experiencing financial problems.

The time of clients, customers, and prospects belongs to them, not to salespeople. If they want to see salespeople at 7:00 A.M. or at 6:00 P.M., the salespeople should accommodate to their needs. Customers and clients should never be viewed as adversaries, but as the means by which salespeople can maintain a livelihood and achieve success. Serving clients and customers is not a burden, but a privilege.

Unfortunately, many business executives fail to teach their people the values of flexibility and accommodation. Salespeople need lessons on how to achieve success, and they need to be taught by individuals with experience in sales, not in accounting or financial management.

In their zeal to squeeze pennies, too many companies have forgotten how to take care of and adapt to their customers. Although they may achieve short-term results, they may be tripping over dollars to pick up nickels.

89

The eyes and hands have it

You can tell a lot about people from the way they use their hands and eyes. "She looks you right in the eye" is usually a compliment.

Why? Because people generally distrust those who periodically avert their gaze, stare at the floor, or become easily distracted by something in the next room. The message of continual eye contact is simple: Someone is taking the time to concentrate on you and your needs.

Good eye contact is critical to successful selling. Staring someone down is never effective, but strong, consistent eye contact gives clients and customers the sense that you not only care about their needs, but that you're sincere in trying to meet them.

A limp handshake can be just as damaging as poor eye contact. Why? Because it implies that you're insincere and uninvolved in the sales process. A firm handshake, in contrast, suggests a person who's involved and in control—not only of his or her own personality and character, but also in control of the sales encounter.

Effective use of the hands and eyes is a critical component of a larger discipline called body language, and few things could be more critical in sales. The advice to sales managers and sales representatives is simple: When you meet a new prospect, client, or customer, give that person a firm and forceful handshake. And when you speak to these people, use your eyes to make them feel as if they're the most important people in the world—whether it's for seconds, minutes, or hours.

Top sales managers and sales representatives are never too proud to practice the skills that will make a difference in their sales performance. That includes proper eye contact and shaking hands.

Meeting Healthcare Challenges

Healthcare is our nation's most dynamic industry—and an incredible force for good.

90

Resist mediocrity

This is one of the most exciting and prosperous periods in the history of American healthcare, but the dominant theme seems to be, "Ain't it awful?"

Angered by escalating healthcare costs, social activists, business executives, and politicians have come down hard on healthcare providers. Even ethicists such as Daniel Callahan, director of the esteemed Hastings Center, are quick to lay blame on the professionals who deliver healthcare services.

A long-time proponent of healthcare rationing, Callahan thinks and talks like a benevolent dictator who understands how the system ought to work and knows what's best for the average American citizen. Convinced that this nation spends far too much on healthcare, Callahan believes that Americans must lower their expectations of the system.

Cost efficiencies, managed care, or government controls will do little to slow down the rise in healthcare costs, according to Callahan. The solution, he believes, is to enter a holding pattern. In other words, stop saving newborns weighing less than 500 grams and limit the use of life-extending technology for people in their 70s and 80s, because, after all, these seniors will probably die anyway.

Callahan believes that it's unreasonable for us to push for new technological and medical advances to improve and extend life and then assume that these technologies can be made available regardless of cost.

"We should make such decisions knowing some lives will be lost," he says. "It will literally be out of the question for society to do everything that might benefit individual patients."

There are no easy 300-word position statements to address these questions. In the years ahead, people like Daniel Callahan will have the ear of leaders in business and politics.

And how can providers respond? By assuming the role of healthcare advocates and developing a clear consensus on national healthcare policy issues.

And what if we fail to take on these new responsibilities? There may be wholesale acceptance of many of Callahan's more radical ideas, leading to a healthcare system founded on mediocrity.

91

Rethink the healthcare system

I n 1989, members of the American College of Healthcare Executives gathered at their annual Congress on Administration to hear Stuart H. Altman, chairman of the Prospective Payment Assessment Commission and a member of the National Leadership Commission on Healthcare—an organization that has recommended establishing a basic level of medical insurance for all Americans.

According to Altman, the prospective payment system has failed in its mission to make hospitals more efficient or slow the rise in healthcare costs. Providers must therefore restructure the healthcare system to ensure its survival.

"We're faced with a system in which all the major participants are struggling," he said. "Patients are confused and nervous about the availability of healthcare, hospitals are losing money, and physicians feel constantly harassed. Yet healthcare costs continue to rise, and private corporations are fed up with paying an increasing percentage of Americans' medical bills."

Altman believes that government and corporations will ultimately force a slowdown in payments to hospitals and therefore recommends system-wide management and budget reforms so that each individual hospital is not left on its own to face inevitable belt-tightening.

He's called for a National Institute for Hospital and Healthcare Productivity to work toward rethinking the healthcare system. In the years ahead, productivity measurement and incentive techniques will play a critical role in the survival of healthcare organizations.

In addition, healthcare executives must rely on creative incentives—not only to address shortages in certain areas, but also to retain strong and capable employees. In spite of his forthright critique, Stuart Altman is no foe of the American healthcare system.

"Both for our healthcare system and our non-healthcare needs, it is very important that this country maintains . . . its private healthcare insurance system," he said. Adopting a variation of the Canadian healthcare system would not only hurt American healthcare, but would also compromise other social programs.

In 1989, a Louis Harris Survey reported that 61 percent of Americans surveyed would trade the American healthcare system for the government-funded healthcare system of Canada. Our healthcare system has a strong track record of success, but we may have failed to present our story in vivid and compelling terms to American healthcare consumers.

Cost-containment strategies, productivity measurement and monitoring, and incentive techniques will yield many benefits, but treating our patients as valued customers and communicating with them on a regular basis may be our ace in the hole.

92

Stick to the basics—I

D avid Williamson was vice chairman of Hospital Corporation of America when he died of cancer in 1986. Past president of the Federation of American Hospitals, he was the recipient of that organization's Individual of the Year Award—an honor accorded to only three people in the last twenty years.

As past president of the Virginia Hospital Association, he was chosen as that organization's Distinguished Man of the Year. And for three years, Dave served on the board of trustees of the American Hospital Association.

But these honors and tributes were hardly the essence of Dave Williamson. Like so many others, he unfurled his true colors as he fought the last and fiercest battle of his life. Shortly before he died, he spent close to an hour with me. The pain he experienced was all too evident. He was candid and direct about his disease, but there was no talk of giving up. He talked about the stresses that healthcare executives face in their jobs, and then he turned the conversation toward "getting back to basics."

Even when he was close to death, Dave remained concerned about the industry to which he had given a significant portion of his life. His point of view was simple: He thought that too many vendors and providers had strayed from the core of healthcare and had forgotten the fundamentals. "There's too much diversification, too much experimentation, and not enough blocking and tackling," he said. "If this industry doesn't start getting back to what it does best, which is delivering quality healthcare, we're headed for lots of problems."

I think about Dave from time to time, and when I do, the words of a friend usually come to mind. Years ago, he told me that there are three things in life that really count: love of family, love of friends, and love of work. Dave Williamson epitomized all three.

Instead of waiting for change, he made change happen. He cared about this industry, and he cared about people—and he had good sense to never stray from the basics.

93

Stick to the basics—II

The healthcare industry should never repeat anything that
resembles the diversification mania of the early 1980s.
But the reasons for executive shoot-from-the-hip reac-
tions were understandable.

Hospitals faced declining occupancy and major changes in
reimbursement. In a defensive strategy, they rejected the
traditions of healthcare and appropriated the teachings of
graduate schools of business. What had been successful in
other industries, they surmised, would also meet with success
in healthcare.

But they were wrong. Many healthcare organizations diversified for diversification's sake. They failed to understand
what diversification was supposed to accomplish. Nor had
they invested time in conducting basic research and in developing a sound marketing plan.

The results were disastrous and laughable. One hospital
bought a racetrack. Another purchased a fast-food restaurant.
Yet another bought a gambling casino. But the big question
was and continues to be, Why?

The reality is that many providers panicked. They had
listened to the doom-and-gloomers predict that 1,000 hospitals would close by 1990, and they didn't want to be one of
them.

Other providers took a different tack. They started
health maintenance organizations and built ambulatory
care centers, surgicenters, nursing homes, and other projects, studying the market-area demographics to ensure

services were necessary and could turn a profit.

The scenario was different, but the results were the same. In the rush to find a solution to their dilemma, healthcare executives had forgotten their primary business and their key strengths. They bought the sad and timeworn cliche that "management is management" and that you can easily transfer skills and experiences from one business or industry to another.

But running a race track, fast-food restaurant, or Atlantic City casino doesn't qualify you to run a hospital, nursing home, or home-care agency. Diversification can be an effective and worthwhile strategy—if it emanates from the hospital's core business and if solid business and marketing plans are developed in advance.

The most prudent advice is to stick to your core business, return to the basics, and keep things simple. Taking care of the sick and helping our patients to stay healthy and well people is our basic mission—and it is one we can take pride in.

94

Mission, vision, and values

In recent years, many providers have remained preoccupied—sometimes obsessed—with financial viability, competition, and marketing. Unfortunately, critical issues such as mission, vision, and values have taken a back seat and, in some cases, have been abandoned in pursuit of a better bottom line.

Corporate America is guilty of a similar myopia. When the conversation turns to managed care, business executives invariably seem more concerned with costs rather than quality. Their highest priority: to squeeze out reductions in high insurance premiums.

Insurance carriers, on the other hand, are only too happy to develop new managed-care plans that meet one objective: to reduce costs. The quality of care delivered by these cost-reducing plans is rarely mentioned.

But business isn't entirely to blame. Most executives want to provide adequate healthcare benefits to their employees at a reasonable price and must control escalating costs. Healthcare insurance costs can reduce or even wipe out a company's bottom line.

More enlightened business executives look for guidance on developing cost-effective benefits packages that deliver on quality.

The cost of healthcare is a critical issue, but everyone in this business—providers, employers, physicians, carriers, and even journalists—needs to remember the business we're in: caring for the sick and keeping people well. Too many of us have forgotten who we are, where we're headed, and what we believe in—our mission, vision, and values.

95

Let's keep the public from getting sick

The cover headline on a 1989 issue of *Newsweek* magazine asked, "Can you afford to get sick?" For the majority of Americans who have employer-sponsored healthcare insurance, the answer is yes.

Unfortunately, escalating health insurance premiums have compelled employers either to share a greater portion of healthcare costs with employees or, in some cases, to cease providing healthcare benefits entirely. At the same time, Medicare and Medicaid fail to offer the coverage that politicians had promised when the programs were conceived.

Many Americans have no understanding of healthcare costs, because the healthcare industry has failed in its mission to provide a clear and direct explanation. There is much they need to learn, but one of the simplest pieces of advice is this: By investing a half-hour per day in health-enhancing activities, people not only prolong their lives, but also reduce their healthcare premiums.

One of the most highly publicized programs to contain healthcare costs is sponsored by Quaker Oats. In the early 1980s, executives responded to 20 to 30 percent increases in healthcare costs by installing a fitness center at corporate headquarters.

Before the program began, Quaker had an average of 769 sick days logged for every 1,000 employees. In 1988, that figure had been reduced 58 percent to 325 days. But Quaker

Oats doesn't stop there. As a reward to employees who help keep annual increases in healthcare costs to slightly more than 5 percent, management offers bonuses.

The story is being repeated in corporations throughout the nation. Johnson & Johnson's "Live for Life" wellness program is so successful that management contracts it out to other organizations.

According to the Leonard Davis Institute of Health Economics at the University of Pennsylvania's Wharton School of Business, programs such as Live for Life could save companies more than 40 percent in healthcare costs.

When the American people learn that responsible wellness and health promotion not only extends lives but also puts money back into their pockets, they will respond. If employers and healthcare organizations take the challenge, billions could be taken off this nation's healthcare bill.

96

Experience the promise
of an aging population

Some of our greatest opportunities will take place in
providing care for an aging population. By the year 2030,
the number of adults over 65 will comprise 21 percent
of the population, up from just 11 percent in 1984.

And consider the numbers: In 1984, 28 million Americans
were 65 or older, but by the year 2000, 34.9 million—13
percent of the population—will be 65 or older. And by 2030,
there will be 65 million Americans 65 or older.

These statistics are even more astounding when considered in light of what the healthcare system has achieved in the
twentieth century. In 1984, the 65-to-74 age group numbered 16.7 million—more than seven times larger than in
1900. The 74-to-84 age group numbered 8.6 million—11
times more than in 1900. And the 85-and-older age group
numbered 2.7 million—21 times larger than in 1900.

The bottom line is that people in this nation are living
longer and healthier, and much of the credit goes to our
healthcare system. And all evidence points to the conclusion
that people will live even longer in the years ahead.

In the next century, people may live to age 90. Age 65 will
be considered middle age, and working until age 75 will be
viewed as typical. According to Age Wave, a healthcare research and consulting firm in Emeryville, California, those
over 65 consume more than a third of healthcare resources
and account for 41 percent of all hospital days.

By the turn of the century Americans over 65 will account for 58 percent of all hospital days and approximately half of all healthcare expenditures. At that time the over-55 population will account for 75 percent of all healthcare spending.

In 1987, the American College of Healthcare Executives and Arthur Andersen Company asked 1,600 healthcare experts to forecast trends within the healthcare industry. The majority of experts predicted that between now and 1995, the aging of the population would have a greater impact on the healthcare industry than any other issue.

There's little doubt that the graying of America will offer the healthcare industry a variety of new and exciting business opportunities. Unfortunately, a disturbing number of providers, vendors, and consultants have yet to awaken to this incredible potential.

97

Promote the good news about healthcare

How can you make money in publishing? The advice is simple: Publish the bad news, and ignore the good news.

Pick up any newspaper or magazine, and you get the impression that we're about to fall off the edge of the earth. Consider the business literature—from *What's Next: How to Prepare Yourself for the Crash of '89* to *Crisis Investing—Opportunities and Profits in the Coming Great Depression.*

And then there's Myron Kandel's book, *How to Cash in on the Coming Stock Market Boom,* and the book that Gary Schilling wrote with Kiril Sokoloff: *Is Inflation Ending? Are You Ready?*

What's the most intriguing point about these books? Kandel's book came out prior to one of the greatest bull markets in history, and Schilling accurately foretold lower inflation—a basic investment theme of the decade. Although both books were accurate, both were also flops in the publishing world.

But Paul Erdman was different. He understood the time-tested formula for publishing success: focus on the negative. Erdman spoke from experience: He wrote his first book from a Swiss prison, where he was incarcerated after a bank he headed went bust. As author of such depressing pieces of fiction as *The Crash of '89, The Last Days of America,* and *The Panic of '89,* Erdman relishes his reputation for making readers squirm. *What's Next?*, another Erdman book, sold 100,000 copies and presented a dismal forecast of economic crisis in 1989. When his predictions failed to materialize, he admitted his error in judgment. "The recession is starting later than I thought . . . and the financial consequences won't be as severe as I had thought," he said.

But the all-time prize for doom-and-gloom goes to Ravi Batra, who penned *The Great Depression of 1990* in 1983 and sold 500,000 copies. Following a natural inclination to capitalize on success, Batra returned in 1987 with another book, *Surviving the Great Depression of 1990*. Although the book sold more than 200,000 copies and is now in paperback, we now know that 1990 passed without a great depression.

The lessons: Write a positive, clear, logical, and accurate book, and you may be faced with a financial flop. Is it any wonder that self-styled pundits and modern-day soothsayers get away with predicting everything from the decline of free enterprise to the end of American healthcare as we know it? And is it any wonder that it's become almost impossible for us to separate reality from make-believe?

The solution is simple: Every major player in the healthcare industry needs to turn away from these negative and sensationalistic writings and seek out an accurate assessment of reality. Or will we be doomed to listen forever to a litany of complaints about America's healthcare system? There's so much we can take pride in. If we refuse to stand up and speak out for our industry, the doom-and-gloomers may well bring about the Armageddon of American healthcare.

98

Recognize the promise of the healthcare industry

Pick up the newspaper. Biotechnology companies are getting ready to sell a new class of products that will increase the ability of physicians to detect and diagnose cancer, heart conditions, and other illnesses.

According to research experts, other products will be able to detect a variety of other illnesses—from infections to hardening of the arteries. The message of hope and optimism is also evident in the area of organ transplants. "Kidney transplants free patients from dialysis treatment, both improving their quality of life and saving medical costs," according to a 1989 issue of *The Wall Street Journal*.

As William H. Frist, director of the heart transplant program at Vanderbilt University Medical Center, Nashville, Tennessee, observed: "It works." The same phenomenon is occurring with such organs as the liver, pancreas, and lungs.

Hospitals are closing, and tough times lie ahead. But in 1988 more hospitals opened than closed in twenty-five of the fifty states. The truth is that when a hospital closes, another facility—such as a women's center or long-term care facility— goes up in its place.

Healthcare is our nation's most dynamic industry and an incredible force for good. Consider the lives saved and the hearts mended. The fastest growing population segment in this country is the 85-plus age group, and there's no more compelling evidence that healthcare has delivered on its promise: longer life. No industry offers greater hope for the future.

99

Appreciate the everyday miracles of healthcare

The healthcare industry works miracles every day. In 1987, I spoke at the annual dinner of a California rehabilitation hospital.

Among the honorees was a young man who had suffered a traumatic brain injury in a car accident. Although several physicians told his parents that he would never return to "regular society," he ultimately regained his driver's license and returned to college.

Another honoree was a vivacious, athletic teenager when her car was hit by a drunk driver. Although she remained comatose for a long time, she eventually learned to get around with a walker and care for her own needs.

A third honoree was a young mother who suffered from Guillain-Barre syndrome, a rare nervous disorder that leaves its victims almost totally paralyzed. After a few months of treatment at the rehabilitation facility, the mother returned to her children and to a normal life.

This rehabilitation hospital wasn't unique in its ability to foster recovery and reentry into the mainstream of life. These human miracles occur routinely, and stories such as these are repeated daily in healthcare facilities across the nation.

Behind each success you'll almost always find a team of disciplined, concerned healthcare professionals who truly care about their patients. Whenever I listen to the clever or cynical remarks of a financial wizard, consultant, or self-styled industry expert, I wonder how much they understand the incredible legacy of this industry.

How many of them will ever know what it takes to salvage the lives of a 35-year-old mother who's suffered a stroke, and a 16-year-old girl who will never walk again? We need to take pride in what we do and in the miracles that we're able to work.

100

Fight the myths of the healthcare industry

Healthcare executives need to take the lead in fighting the myths and stereotypes that have the potential of destroying this industry and the people who work in it. Following are some of the most popular:

✦ Industry is shutting down. Hospital closings are inevitable.

No matter what the industry, not every organization can sustain the pace set by increased competition. Some healthcare organizations have been victims of poor management, while others were never planned to deliver healthcare services in the current environment.

But other organizations have adapted to new demands with innovative products and services and, in some cases, they're prospering.

✦ Healthcare is no place for a creative business person.

Some of the most dynamic, forward-thinking, creative business leaders in America today are working in the healthcare industry. "Some of the most positive, stunning, creative things taking place in American business today are occurring here in the tumult of healthcare," said Ron Zemke, co-author of *Service America*.

"I'm convinced that there are so many opportunities and so much is going on that we'll see some of the most creative managers and creative work in management in general in the next ten years—not from high tech, but from this industry."

✦ Hospitals are experiencing DRG (diagnostic-related group) crunch and are showing a poor bottom line.

Some hospitals are under the gun, but others are making more money than at any time in their history. Why? Because they've streamlined their operations and diversified into other businesses. Healthcare executives are running these institutions like business-minded enterprises, not disoriented charities.

✦ Physicians are losing power and prestige.

The opposite is more likely. Hospitals now realize that without the loyalty and support of physicians, few patients will use their institutions. Healthcare executives therefore view physicians as their number one customers—the primary gatekeepers for this highly competitive industry.

✦ For-profit hospitals are growing rapidly.

After World War II, for-profit hospitals were about 18 percent of the total hospital universe. As of 1987, they were only 13 percent, and this figure may continue to drop during the 1990s. Some experts even predict that for-profit chains will have all but disappeared in five to ten years.

✦ For-profit hospitals bring in more profits than not-for-profits.

The reality is that some not-for-profit hospitals have been known to have a profit ratio of more than 16 percent, while for-profit hospitals can't even get into that ballpark. Many corporations outside the healthcare industry marvel at the bottom-line profitability of hospitals.

✦ Vendors are having a tough time surviving in the new healthcare environment.

Examples abound of healthcare vendors and consulting firms who recently racked up the finest sales and performance records in years. The time-tested solution is simple: an ongoing presence in the field, coupled with aggressive selling.

101

Do your homework

In the mid-1980s, building senior-housing facilities was considered a boom field, ripe for development and making big bucks.

Every journal article and research report pointed to the aging of America. Nursing homes were overflowing, and retirees were moving in great numbers to Florida, Arizona, California, and South Carolina. All the conditions seemed right, but along the way, many of these developers lost sight of the basics.

For example, lifecare centers were places where seniors could retire and receive care for the rest of their lives. Although some were run like luxury hotels, most were a series of studio apartments where active seniors could retire with other people of a similar age and interests. If they later became incapacitated, they could receive care in a nearby nursing home.

Unfortunately, the lifecare concept turned sour for many of its developers. Developers had based their initial financial projections on turnover among residents, but the people who entered lifecare centers stayed for many, many years. To the surprise of many developers, the senior residents failed to die on schedule.

And now another phenomenon is occurring. A growing number of retirees don't move, choosing instead to remain in old neighborhoods with friends and families.

This emerging trend has also been a shock to developers of senior housing, who assumed that everyone over age 55 would want to relocate to a warmer climate.

Where did most developers of senior housing projects fall short? They failed to do their homework in the form of basic demographic and psychographic research. They neglected to develop sound marketing and business plans. But most of all, they were victims of every popular myth and stereotype about seniors.

In assuming that all seniors had the same interests and wanted to pursue retirement living in the same way, they lost out on significant business opportunities. The reality is that the senior market is as diverse as numerous younger markets. Senior citizens pursue varied lifestyles and interests, and they can never be lumped together in one market.

For developers, it was a tough and expensive mistake—one that could have been avoided through careful planning and research.

102

Don't be seduced
by the numbers

We're living in an age of statistics. Hardly a day goes by without the results of a new study being announced in which researchers and statisticians have had yet another field day. Government and private agencies present mind-boggling amounts of data at seminars and conventions and before congressional committees.

What does it mean? Simply that the healthcare industry is being researched to death. Research has its place. Most of us want to discover new facts or get confirmation and validation for what we already believe. But some of these pedants and bean counters often lack a critical element in their research: people—independent, stubborn, creative, contrary, loving, feeling, and often unpredictable people.

Consider how consumers responded to the introduction of the new "Coke" in 1985. And what about the security analysts who predicted high interest rates and a sluggish stock market in 1986? And in our own healthcare industry, how do you account for facilities that rose from the brink of death and are now flourishing—thanks to the people who ran them?

The truth is that problem solving and decision making are neater and tidier if you ignore or minimize the role of people. Conduct a study, analyze the numbers, and make a logical decision. It sounds simple enough, but fortunately, we don't always behave in accordance with researchers' predictions and theories.

And what does this mean for healthcare? Don't believe all the studies, statistics, graphs, and pie charts. In times like these, it would be easy for executives, vendors, and consultants to believe the soothsayers of doom and gloom and retreat.

Fortunately, other providers and suppliers have taken the opposite tack and are now more aggressive than ever. Their prize: not just survival, but greater market share.

103

Innovate within the context of your main mission

Catch phrases rise and fall with the fashions of the times, but one reverberates like a constant refrain: "Let's get back to basics."

"We've gotten away from the very things that made us so successful," said the CEO of a large for-profit hospital chain. "And that's delivering quality healthcare."

He bemoaned the fact that healthcare executives had strayed from their foundations and, in doing so, had gotten involved in costly business experiments. "It was a mistake," he added. "But now we're focusing and getting back to what we do best: delivering cost-efficient, quality healthcare. That's our mission, and we had better pay attention to what we do well or we'll lose our franchise in the industry."

In a conversation several weeks later, the CEO of a hotel chain reiterated the theme: "I'm spending all my time getting rid of about forty ancillary businesses that just aren't the things we do best or know anything about," he moaned. "Our business is delivering clean, comfortable rooms to our guests and making sure that we get their repeat business. But boy, did we get off the track."

Fortunately, business decision making is changing. Throughout the healthcare industry, executives, vendors, and consultants have come to appreciate the wisdom of a back-to-basics approach to business. Vendors and consultants are letting salespeople in on the realities of the healthcare marketplace and developing products that help providers save money and make money.

In the same way, healthcare organizations have put together well-trained, knowledgeable sales teams who promote products that are attuned to the needs of healthcare consumers.

You don't have to be a genius to realize that there's plenty of opportunity in the healthcare business, but that all of us need to stick to our knitting. And what does that mean? Keep it simple, and do what you do best. Sell quality products and services to a flourishing, dynamic marketplace that's hungry for creative solutions.

104

Play it straight and open with the media

Debs Myers was the antithesis of the polished New York City public relations agency executive. Shaped like a football, he wore rumpled suits that seemed to be bought for someone else.

He chain-smoked so many cigars that you could follow him by his trail of ashes. He was incorrigible—the quintessential character—but he knew the media, and he knew public relations.

When I first met Debs, I was communications director for the American Medical Association. Every other day a newspaper, magazine, or television news program presented the AMA as the victimizer—and it was no wonder. For years, the AMA had ignored the press and played hide-and-seek with reporters.

Why? It was simple: The AMA looked at all journalists as the enemy, and concluded that little would be gained—and much could be lost—by cooperating with them.

Debs pursued a deceptively simple turnaround strategy with the press. He asked AMA officials to meet with the press and explain their positions on a variety of issues. He visited with the news directors of the major television and radio networks and with the editorial boards of newspapers and magazines.

Simply stated, he unlocked the doors of the AMA to reporters. Many news organizations that had taken positions against the AMA began to call its offices to seek out physicians for interviews.

"Good public relations or press relations are simply good common sense, but too many people get confused," Debs said.

He was right. Too many organizations—and that includes consulting firms, providers, and vendors—treat the media as adversaries. Executives continue to dodge and hide from reporters, and organizations still stonewall. Otherwise intelligent and educated people speak to reporters with no clear objective in mind and then deny or protest their remarks when they appear in print.

The press can be an asset to any organization. But media relations is an ongoing process and a two-way street. Executives should speak to the media openly and honestly and give journalists the time, attention, and respect they deserve.

Despite popular stereotypes, many reporters who work in the trade press are rational in their approach, moderate to conservative in their politics, and respectful of quality management. Providers, consulting firms, and vendors can go a long way by developing a sound but simple media relations strategy: Use patience, judgment, and common sense in dealing with the press. Treat journalists as skilled professionals who know their business.

105

Fitness means everything

Ron Jaworski was a wily, scrambling quarterback with the Philadelphia Eagles and the Miami Dolphins. An accomplished athlete, Jaworski understood the importance of keeping fit.

When Tom Kean, governor of Jaworski's home state of New Jersey, tried to eliminate high school physical education courses, Jaworski lashed out. Physical education has always been a tempting target for politicians, who claim that school budgets should further academic pursuits—not running, football, or tennis.

Under veiled threats to hold back on promised pay increases, teachers and school principals have often caved in to physical education cuts. Ironically, many of the politicians who demean physical education also bemoan the high cost of healthcare.

The health outlook for this country's children is grim, according to a 1989 report from the American Alliance for Health, Physician Education, Recreation, and Dance. Forty percent of children between the ages of 5 and 8 already exhibit obesity, elevated blood pressure, high cholesterol, and inactivity—all risks for coronary artery disease, according to the study.

In addition, 50 percent of our nation's children fail to get exercise adequate enough to develop healthy hearts and lungs. Additional research is equally discouraging. Only 60 percent of boys between the ages of 6 and 12 could do more than one chin-up, and 25 percent failed to do any, according to a 1985 report from the University of Michigan Institute of Social Research. Among girls between the ages of 6 and 12, 70 percent could do only one chin-up, and more than half failed to do any.

Exercise improves overall health and well-being. If this nation is truly committed to reducing the high costs of healthcare, how can we deny an investment in quality physical education for our children? We should focus on the benefits of physical education for everyone—from the young mother and her daughter, to the grandfather and his grandson.

Some of the most innovative and far-sighted corporations in this country have already learned that helping employees take better care of themselves is more than positive public relations—it makes good business sense.

The future of this nation rests with its young people. Unless we help them take personal responsibility for their own health and well-being, no amount of government regulation will influence healthcare costs.

106

Look before you leap

In 1988, I addressed the Massachusetts Hospital Association. Preceding me on the program was the lieutenant governor of the commonwealth, Evelyn Murphy, who was credited with helping Governor Michael Dukakis obtain passage of the Massachusetts Health Security Act.

This act required businesses with more than five employees to provide health insurance for most workers by 1992. Michael Dukakis was never elected president of the United States, and the Massachusetts Health Security Act never became a prototype for a comprehensive national healthcare plan.

But Dukakis' love affair with the Canadian healthcare system has spread to other sectors of our population to become a topic of widespread discussion and debate.

Is Canada's healthcare system really a diamond in the rough? Or has it begun to unravel, in the mold of the British healthcare system? Recent evidence suggests disappointment, missed opportunities, and a general breakdown of the system.

Michael A. Walker, executive director of the Fraser Institute in Vancouver, British Columbia, has chronicled deficiencies within the Canadian system. According to Walker, Canadians have experimented with health maintenance organizations and preferred provider organizations to sustain service levels and contain costs. But under the Canadian system, such choices as the number of physicians who can practice medicine are severely restricted.

And there are other problems.

✦ Waiting periods for elective surgeries are commonplace; at a large metropolitan hospital in British Columbia, the average wait for elective surgery is four weeks. Lines for cardiac bypass operations grow longer—not shorter—and patients sometimes die before they can be scheduled for surgery. Some women must wait up to two and one-half months for a mammogram.

✦ In Newfoundland, there's one CT scanner for almost 600,000 citizens. In British Columbia, there are seven CT scanners for 4.6 million residents, while across the border in Seattle—a city which has one-tenth of British Columbia's population—there are 17. In all of Canada, there are four lithotripters, or one for every 6.3 million people, while in the U.S. there are 228, or one for every 1.1 million people.

✦ Work stoppages among Canadian healthcare workers are centered on the quality of care able to be delivered and lack of funds to purchase up-to-date technology.

As more Canadians take advantage of their healthcare system, costs have begun to escalate. At present, Canada spends approximately 8 percent of its gross national product on healthcare, compared to 11 percent in the United States.

In its attempt to contain costs, Canada is rationing through waiting lines. The United States, in contrast, is working to contain costs by offering alternate means of care, such as freestanding clinics, managed-care plans, and health-promotion programs.

The U.S. healthcare system has met every challenge it has been given and has performed with distinction. Although escalating healthcare costs, long-term care for the aged, and access to care are serious problems, we should take care before we abandon a largely excellent healthcare system simply to improve the bottom lines of a few corporations.

Before social activists and government bureaucrats drive home the case for Canadian healthcare, they should consider the following points:

✦ The United States has approximately ten times the population of Canada.

✦ Americans look with disfavor on excessive government intervention. They know from experience the nightmare of government bureaucracy and the inefficiencies of such government-operated agencies as the post office.

✦ Two-thirds of the United States population does not yet have adequate health insurance, but still wants access to quality healthcare and high technology.

✦ Most of the physicians in this country are entrepreneurial.

What's my advice? Don't be too quick to listen to the propagandists who use Canada and England as shining examples of how healthcare should be reconfigured in the United States. Before you take sides and conclude that these nations offer a magic panacea to our system's ills, take a look at what's really happening.

These facts, and the troubling question of where we would find the money to finance such a mammoth endeavor, lead to a single conclusion: Universal health insurance coverage along the lines of the Canadian system will not happen in the United States.

107

Stand up and fight

At age 13, I was enrolled in high school in Buffalo, New York. It was a decent school, but it still had its share of bad characters, including a tough bully of a kid named Billy.

Billy was a mean-spirited kid who got his kicks from pushing me around and calling me names. After weeks of this routine, I punched Billy in the nose. He backed off for a few days, but soon he was back, with more bullying and name calling.

So the next time he came at me, I hit him three times. And that was the last I heard from Billy. He never bothered me again.

Every industry in America has a Billy. For the past decade, the healthcare industry has tried to cooperate with the federal government and Congress through rational, deliberate, and constructive discussion. But what have been the results of these slow, painful negotiations? Between 1981 and 1988, Medicare and Medicaid were cut by $37 million, and there are ongoing proposals to cut even greater sums.

Medicare and Medicaid were initiated to provide care for the elderly and medically indigent—a problem that hasn't declined but accelerated. Because of these budget cuts, some rural and public hospitals might close their doors.

The healthcare industry is notorious for its ability to tolerate pain and abuse, but now the time has come to punch back. The solution is in grass roots aggressiveness. Healthcare providers and their allies need to confront local, state, and national political representatives with some hard realities.

Consider, for example, how many people work in healthcare institutions—not just the 6,000 healthcare executives, but also the millions of service workers in such needed areas as housekeeping, maintenance, laboratories, or respiratory therapy.

If exposed to similar abuse and criticism, other industries would have launched massive protests and public relations campaigns. The healthcare industry has been pushed as far as it can be, and now is the time to punch back.

108

The bright future
of healthcare

The American public loves to hear about the future—not just what's going to happen, but how they can get ready for it—now.

Let's face it, there's an incredible vacuum in national healthcare leadership. The national associations and professional societies aren't doing their job—and maybe that's why the public is so confused and angry.

There may be a lot of problems out there, but there are also a lot of opportunities. In fact, change rings opportunity. Just think about the aging of America. Sure, it's going to be tough, but think about what this means for the healthcare system: a whole new model of care, centered not on treating the acutely ill, but on treating the chronically ill.

According to Jeff Goldsmith, by the mid-1990s, coronary bypass surgery will be a sunset technology. Instead, we'll see screening technologies like ultrasound, cinematic MR, and laser angioplasty. The same scenario applies to cancer. By the mid-1990s, we'll have genetic screening, and we'll be able to substitute genetic information or alter its expression.

So what does this mean? The bottom line is that we'll be facing new enemies: Alzheimer's disease, arthritis, and Parkinson's disease will be our adversaries. And we'll be evolving a whole new way of doing business. Instead of just treating organs, we'll be treating patients and families. Instead of grappling with single episodes of illness, we'll be trying to

229

restructure a patient's life. Instead of facing high episodic costs, we'll be facing low unit costs and high life-cycle costs. Instead of relying on surgeons and medical staff specialists, we'll be turning to primary care physicians.

Finally, instead of delivering care in the hospital, we'll be coming directly to the doors of private homes. It doesn't take a genius to realize that we're headed for a new era of medicine—one where we try to avoid inpatient care and focus on independent living.

109

Support long-range investments in good health

National health insurance will stem the tide of escalating healthcare costs. At least that's what you hear from some political pundits.

But where's the evidence that the government will deliver on its promises? The healthcare system of the Veterans Administration has been rocked by scandal in recent years. And although they were created out of a sincere desire to help the indigent, Medicare and Medicaid programs are mired in bureaucratic nonsense.

In 1989, the Amateur Athletic Union and Chrysler Corporation released a study establishing that young people between the ages of 10 and 13 are not only getting fatter, but also have less physical stamina. Why? Mechanized transportation and video games may have created a new generation of miniature couch potatoes.

What's the solution? The answer is obvious: If this nation truly wants to reduce healthcare costs, then Uncle Sam should declare war on our sedentary, destructive lifestyles. At minimum, we could put a dent in the hundreds of billions of dollars spent on illness by making a commitment to exercise, stop smoking, eat right, and control our consumption of alcohol.

This Herculean effort won't be easy, and we couldn't do it alone. Washington bureaucrats and corporate executives would need the support and participation of schools, providers, physicians, nurses and, of course, healthcare consumers.

But we can take first steps by working within homes and schools—and ultimately reaching every man, woman, and child in this nation. If we truly want to get a handle on healthcare costs, we have to reward good health.

110

Focus on quality and service

The terms *quality* and *service* are more than catchwords in an expensive four-color brochure. Instead, quality and service are principles that must be integrated into the sales and service strategy and business operations of every successful vendor and consulting firm.

In recent years, providers have become more skeptical and angry about low-priced but inferior products and services offered by vendors and consulting firms. In the early 1980s, providers were duped by opportunistic vendors and consultants who tried to capitalize on cost-containment paranoia and the panic brought on by changes in Medicare reimbursement. Diagnostic-related groups (DRGs) meant hospitals were reimbursed by Medicare for the patient's diagnosis, rather than for expenses incurred during treatment.

Fortunately, astute and experienced providers soon woke up to the fact that buying products and services on the basis of price alone usually resulted in additional money spent on malfunctions and breakdowns.

In the end, the price was far greater than if they had originally purchased quality products at a higher price from a service-oriented vendor.

But there were other problems. Some providers purchased good-quality products at reasonable prices from reputable vendors, but neglected to read the service contracts. Although many vendors had not yet become service conscious, providers soon ers soon forced the issue by insisting on strong contracts, follow-through, and value-added services.

Price continues to be an important criterion, but vendors and consultants can no longer assume that a low price will make a sale.

The ingredients for success are simple. Start with quality products and services that your sales force understands and believes in and that providers can count on. Demonstrate your commitment to not only deliver good service, but also to monitor service performance.

Quality and service are the key words of the healthcare industry, and vendors and consulting firms who successfully deliver on both counts will see their sales curves rise.

111

Be positive about the future and proud of the past

Listen to television and read popular newspapers and magazines, and you might easily conclude that American society is on the brink of disaster.

Gerhard Stock, a German free-lance writer, said that watching the American parade was "like watching a lion go around with an inferiority complex." The rest of the world continues to revel in the American dream, according to Stock.

"One can lose or maybe forget a dream. But a good dream lives on one way or the other," he said. "We can tell. After the war, when we were down on our knees, the Americans not only didn't send us to hell but helped us up and even offered us their friendship. Thus, their dream is very powerful and convincing. It won believers here, too, and very persistent ones; we were never able to deny its reality."

Stock concludes with a plea: America must not surrender its dream, because so many people look to this nation as a symbol of hope and promise.

The American healthcare system is still the envy of the world's nations, who look to us for direction and leadership. With all of its faults, and despite ongoing criticism from insurance carriers, corporations, and the government, the system performs well—every day of the year. It's easy for self-appointed gurus and pundits to suggest that the United

States pattern its healthcare system after Canada. But are these people aware that the number of Americans who are age 65 or older exceeds the total population of Canada?

The underlying reality is that people are living longer. And that demographic shift is creating massive disruptions within the actuarial tables of insurance companies, corporate healthcare benefits, pension funds, and Medicaid and Medicare.

The healthcare industry should receive kudos—not insults—for extending life and increasing its quality. Unfortunately, that's not the story you hear from government, business, insurance companies, the popular press, and even the healthcare industry.

The message is clear: Providers must remind the American people of the value they receive from the healthcare industry. If people knew and understood the truth about healthcare, they would be less inclined to accept the disparaging remarks of self-styled experts. Above all, we can never surrender our dreams or optimism about the future.